CW01023039

*"The face of
Truth is
covered with a
golden veil.
Uncover that
Reality,
Pushan, to the
glance of one
devoted to
Truth."*
                    Ishopanishad

Yoga the Sacred Science
volume one

SAMADHI
The Highest State of Wisdom

Yoga the Sacred Science
volume one

Swami Rama

Himalayan Institute Hospital Trust
Swami Rama Nagar, P.O. Doiwala,
Distt. Dehradun - 248140, Uttaranchal, India

Acknowledgments

We would like to express our appreciation to Connie Gage for designing the cover, and to Wesley Van Linda for the many services rendered in producing this book.

Editing: Barbara Bova
         Kay Gendron

Cover design: Connie Gage

© 2002 by the Himalayan Institute Hospital Trust
First USA edition, 2002
Printed in the United States of America
ISBN 8-188157-01-5
Library of Congress Control Number 2002105324

Published by:

Himalayan Institute Hospital Trust
Swami Rama Nagar, P.O. Doiwala,
Distt. Dehradun - 248140, Uttaranchal, India
Tel: 91-135-412068, Fax: 91-135-412008
hihtsrc@sancharnet.in; www.hihtindia.org

Distributed by:
Lotus Press
P.O. Box 325
Twin Lakes, WI 53181
www.lotuspress.com
lotuspress@lotuspress.com
800-824-6396

ALL RIGHTS RESERVED. No part of this book may be reproduced in any form or by any electronic or mechanical means including information storage and retrieval systems without permission in writing from the publisher, except by a reviewer who may quote brief passages in a review.

Table of Contents

Preface

In 1977 the headquarters of the Himalayan International Institute of Yoga Science and Philosophy was located in Glenview, Illinois, near Chicago. At that time Swami Rama lived at the Institute and was everything to us — guru and loving teacher, father and disciplinarian as required, and the dearest friend one could ever hope to find — "us" being about twenty-five ashramites, living and working and studying under his close guidance. During this period the Institute began an innovative graduate program in Eastern studies. A few of us were allowed to enroll in one course in the graduate school, provided we maintained our other duties. We, of course, chose the course on the yoga sutras that Swamiji was teaching. Of all Swamiji's lectures and seminars that I have had the opportunity to attend over a period of twenty years, none of them made as lasting an impression as the lectures of that yoga sutras course. I have never forgotten the excitement and insatiable thirst for knowledge that those lectures inspired. Swamiji played the role of professor impeccably, coming to class with spectacles and pens and lecture notes. He scolded us and teased us for being dullards as we could not put intelligent questions nor give creative answers to his seemingly unending queries. He presented the material with such love and fire and enthusiasm, we felt as though all the secrets of the mysteries of the universe were being revealed to us and that nothing could ever be thought of as impossible again. I felt the same excitement and sense of awe on being given the opportunity to help organize those lectures along with subsequent lectures on the yoga sutras into a book. While working on the manuscript I realized that Swamiji was always teaching us yoga sutras — how to live in the world and apply the sutras in daily life. *Yoga the Sacred Science* is an attempt to present those lectures in a form in which their invaluable content can continue to be utilized and savored for many years to come.

We have tried to preserve the original language so that Swamiji's presence is not veiled. Swamiji's lectures were typically not limited to one topic or to a predictable, chronological orderliness. Rather he was very pragmatic and did not hesitate to introduce whatever subject was most relevant to the needs of the attending audience. He often digressed to relay stories of the experiences of his youth and spiritual training to help clarify or emphasize a particular teaching. This style has been maintained as much as possible throughout the book.

Swamiji frequently reminded us that if we want to understand the yoga sutras, we need to understand every sutra from a practical viewpoint. Over and over he stressed the importance of applying these aphorisms in daily life, and reassured us that we really can practice Patanjali's system of yoga and live in the world; there is no need to retire and live in a monastery or somewhere in the caves of the Himalayas. Accordingly, he emphasized the aspects of those sutras that would be most helpful for us novice students who were just beginning the incredible journey within. Swamiji particularly highlighted the therapeutic value of certain sutras and how to apply them to improve the quality of life. The practicums in methods that are therapeutically helpful — breathing exercises, asanas, concentration, and meditation — that Swamiji shared with us throughout the course of the lectures, have been included.

Patanjali repeatedly emphasized the necessity of understanding and learning to control all aspects of the mind and its modifications as prerequisite to attaining samadhi. According to Swamiji, Patanjali's *Yoga Sutras* are the basis of ancient psychology. Swamiji's description of the totality of the mind, the functions of the mind, and the emotions, goes far beyond the concepts of modern psychology, and provides insight into the intricacies of yoga psychology, making this an invaluable edition from the therapeutic viewpoint as well as its practicality as a guide for living a healthy, balanced life.

As the contents of this book have been taken from lecture courses, it is not intended to be a comprehensive, scholarly commentary on the yoga sutras, nor is it an all-inclusive expansion of all one hundred ninety-six sutras. However, it would be a mistake to think that the material in this book is merely preliminary. As with all of Swamiji's writings and teachings, repeated readings reveal deeper and subtler levels of the knowledge of the science of yoga, according to the reader's level of preparedness. Swamiji emphasized the first four sutras in his lectures, as the first four sutras are the nucleus of the yoga sutras, and the rest of the sutras are the expansion of the first four.

Because the material proved to be too extensive to include in one volume, we have decided to make three volumes of *Yoga the Sacred Science*. The first volume of this narrative adventure into the science of yoga is entitled *Samadhi, The Highest State of Wisdom* because the major theme of the yoga sutras is how to experience the highest state of wisdom, samadhi. The following volume will focus on sadhana and raja yoga, the practical methods for attaining samadhi. Samyama will be the focus of the final volume.

Barbara Bova

The Ultimate Goal of DARSHANA
is to See REALITY

Yoga *darshana* is one of the most ancient
darshanas. The word *darshana* comes from the root
drishyate anena which means, "that through which
you can see." That particular system through which
you can see Reality is called darshana. Just as you
can see yourself in the mirror, so also, through yoga
darshana, the yoga sutras, can you see the Self.
Darshana is not the same thing as philosophy.
Philosophy is a compound word meaning "love for
knowledge." Darshana is not a mere love for
knowledge. This is one difference between oriental
and occidental philosophy: the ultimate goal of
darshana is to see Reality.

Yoga science is based on Samkhya philosophy,
which is the very basis of all sciences. Samkhya
(*samyag akhyate*) means, "that which explains the
whole." Samkhya embraces the whole universe—how
the universe came into existence, and all relationships
within the universe. It explains human life on all
levels—our relationship with the universe, our
relationship with the creator who created the universe
(if there is any), our relationships with our own mind
and our inner being, our relationship with the center
of consciousness, and our very existence. Even if a

person is agnostic or atheist, they will get something from Samkhya philosophy.

The Samkhya philosophy gave birth to mathematics. If there were no mathematics, no one would understand science. All the sciences would crumble if mathematics were removed because science is based on mathematics. Samkhya philosophy is the very basis of yoga science. I am teaching you what I was taught in the monastery by a great swami, Chakravarti, who was a great Indian mathematician. He taught me by drawing triangles, lines, and dots in the sand.

Samkhya philosophy defines the whole process of understanding that which is real and that which is not real. Here the word *Reality* is not used as you use it in the external world. Let us consider the blackboard I am using. Is it real? According to Samkhya philosophy, the blackboard is not real because Reality is that which is not subject to change, death, and decay. It is true that it has a material reality, but the blackboard itself is not real because its form and name can change at any time. If an object's form and name can change, it is not Absolute Reality. According to Samkhya, Reality, or Truth, is that which exists in all three times — the past, present, and future. In the material world, a man of flesh and bones is real, but in Samkhya philosophy, Reality means that which is everlasting, exists in all times, and is not subject to change, death, and decay. The world appears to exist; it appears to be real, but actually it is not because it exists on the existence of something else. Those who do not know Reality, think that the world is real. To those who know Samkhya, the world is not real.

When yoga science was taught to us in the monastery, they always taught *Karika,* a classical text of Buddhism, and Samkhya along with it so it could be more easily understood. *Karika,* Samkhya, and yoga are very closely related to each other. If you want to understand the systems of Indian philosophy, including Buddhism and Jainism, you should study the *Karika.* The *Karika* does not say that one should try to understand God or talk about heaven and hell; it is very practical. The first sutra of the *Karika* is: *dukha-traya-abhighatat:* "Oh man, be aware of the pain that arises from three levels—pain coming from within, pain coming from outside, and pain coming from nature. First gain your freedom from these three sets of pain."

The science of yoga is thousands of years old. Man has always searched for ways to make life happier in the external world. Though he was partially successful, he was not yet truly happy. Then he started searching for an internal way of organizing the internal states. The great sages, with the help of meditation techniques, dived deep into the inner realms of their being and experienced the unspoken great words of wisdom. Some five thousand years ago, when there were no printing presses, the teachings were imparted to students orally in a very compact form called *sutras* so they could be easily remembered. Through practices and experience, the truths given by the teachers could be verified.

Patanjali was a great sage who systematized and organized the study and teachings of yoga. He was not the first teacher of yoga, nor is he considered to be the originator of yoga science. There is a saying in Sanskrit, "One who was born first, the first who came into manifestation, was the first teacher of yoga."

Patanjali was only the codifier of yoga science. His approach is very practical; he was not a simple religious preacher or priest, but a scientist and a great philosopher who understood life with its currents and crosscurrents. He was a great yogi who practiced, who knew, and who made experiments. Patanjali was an enlightened being, a sage, who has given us yoga science for the benefit of all human beings.

After doing his own experiments for a long time, Patanjali organized the study of the internal states into one hundred ninety-six sutras. These sutras are called yoga darshana. The word *sutra* means "a string," and the yoga sutras are connected with each other like the beads of a mala. Patanjali sometimes used several sutras to express the same idea if one sutra was not adequate to completely explain a particular subject. If more than one sutra is used for explaining a particular concept, it means that concept is very essential and should be thoroughly understood.

The *Yoga Sutras* is a very important classical text. I want to give you a glimpse of the whole text. All three schools of Buddhism—Mahayana, Hinayana, and Nirvayana—and the Jain teachings have borrowed from this text. The Upanishads are replete with the teachings of yoga science. Every religion in the world includes something about yoga, yet yoga is not a religion.

Every word of the sutras has meaning, so you need to understand each word properly in order to understand the whole sutra. Sutras are similar to aphorisms in English, but they are not mere aphorisms. They are compact, concise, abstruse sentences that cannot be understood without expansion and explanation. I studied the sutras many times in my childhood, yet I still did not really know much about them. The yoga sutras are not actually meant for students to study because they will drive you crazy! They are really meant as an outline for the teachers. If you study only the sutra as it is, you will not understand what it means. Patanjali intended for the teachers to practice the sutras and to expand on them for students. Understanding has nothing to do with how learned you are. If someone is a very learned person and is knowledgeable about the scriptures but does not practice, it will be very difficult for that person to comprehend the entire concept, philosophy, psychology, and practical aspects of Patanjali. If you do not practice the yoga sutras, you cannot explain them, no matter how much you study, and you will make serious mistakes. Only when you practice the sutras will you understand them very clearly. Only those teachers who are competent, who have studied the tradition from their competent teachers, and who have practiced and applied the truths therein, have the right to teach the yoga sutras. In ancient times only those who were adept taught the sutras. No one would study them from anyone who was not a perfect yogi. Only someone who has practiced this science with mind, action, and speech, and who has traditionally studied this science, can explain and impart the knowledge to those students who are prepared.

The first four sutras are very important. They are the cornerstones of the architecture of yoga science. Patanjali explains the first four sutras of the first chapter in the entire one hundred ninety-six sutras. These four sutras are the nucleus; the rest of the sutras are the explanation.

The four basic sutras are:

Now yoga science is being expounded.

By gaining control over mind and its modifications one can attain the highest state of wisdom or samadhi.

When you come to realize your essential nature, you get freedom.

You are constantly identifying yourself with the objects of the world. That is why you are suffering.

Patanjali did not write these sutras for swamis or renunciates; he meant them for the people of the world so that one can live in the world yet remain unaffected and undisturbed, enjoying peace, happiness, and bliss. Students often ask their teacher for that happiness they can attain themselves by simple methods, by simple ways in life. Don't tell yourself that you cannot have happiness and bliss; you can do that. Don't believe that the external world or the objects of the world can give you peace, happiness, and bliss. Many people are rushing here and there, worrying, and being tossed by the objects of the world. To gain happiness you do not have to run around or go here and there. It is all at your disposal and within your reach. Peace is within you.

Have you determined to find peace, happiness, and bliss? Have you decided to do that? Or are you still searching for someone else who will give you peace, happiness, and bliss? The scriptures say that no one in the world will ever find these goals in any relationship. Peace and happiness are within you, beyond your body, breath, senses, and mind. You can attain that peace by learning how to direct your energies within toward the deeper aspects of your being. To attain that you do not have to retire from the world. You do not have to shun your relationships or abstain from your duties. You only need to discipline yourself. Discipline means not allowing yourself to be dissipated mentally by your thoughts, actions, or speech. Patanjali, the codifier of yoga science, taught that all human beings can attain the goal of human life by understanding the yoga sutras, practicing them, and applying them in daily life.

Yoga is a science, a philosophy, and a psychology. Yoga science deals with the subtleties of life. It offers a practical side to philosophy and provides a variety of techniques. Yoga psychology teaches how to apply yoga science to know yourself. The *Yoga Sutras* of Patanjali are the foundation of ancient psychology, including the Buddhist, Zen, Jain, and other psychology systems that support the seven systems of Indian philosophy. There is no real distinction between Eastern and Western psychology. The actual distinction is between the ancient and modern psychologies. There are many branches of ancient psychology.

The word *psychology* means "the science of mental life," but modern psychology has not developed to the extent where it can truly say that it knows how to study mental life. When you study mind as a subject you are merely collecting the information and opinions of others and trying to study what it is. I never met anyone who could really study my mind, even though I went to well-known psychics. They made various predictions that I did not believe. I said, "Tell me what is going on *now* in my mind and what has happened with me in the past, then I will believe what is going to happen with me in the future."

Modern psychology has really studied only behaviorism. That is not the study of the mind, but only aspects of the mind. Behaviorism is an incomplete science. Very little of the mind is expressed through behavior. Therefore, by studying behavior you cannot understand the totality of the mind. Historically, modern psychology is based on the study of the behavior of mentally abnormal people. Patanjali did not base his science on abnormal behavior, even though he was fully aware of that particular category of mind. Modern psychology was born out of the study of misery, out of trying to understand mental problems that could not be handled by medicines. Modern psychology teaches that we cannot fully understand anyone's thinking process because we cannot really know how someone is thinking. Patanjali studied and analyzed the normal mind in its totality, with all its functions and modifications. Yoga psychology evolved from the prime necessity of attaining realization.

Modern psychology is not yet a finished product. It reaches certain conclusions today, and tomorrow those conclusions are discarded. Besides behaviorism there was another branch of psychology in which such great psychologists as Freud, James, Williams, and Jung tried to understand the deeper aspects of the mind, but they did not thoroughly accomplish this. They did begin to study hypnosis, but did not really go far in their studies of the mind using hypnosis. Self-hypnosis and autosuggestions can help people with problems up to a certain extent, but they cannot lead you to know the deeper levels of life. At this point, the ancient or yoga psychology begins its study.

Ancient psychology explains that the human mind has an immense capacity. If the mind can be prevented from distractions and dissipation, it can be disciplined and directed in the right direction. Yoga psychology is a complete science. Yoga psychology is very deep and can be understood only by practicing it, not by memorizing the yoga sutras. Patanjali's method is subtle, exact, and profound. If modern psychologists fully understood Patanjali's subtle methods, they could do tremendous good for society. But modern psychologists are usually not taught to go beyond the conscious and unconscious fields of the mind, or to become aware of the soul, which is the very goal of human life.

Psychology deals with mental life, both the conscious and unconscious. With the help of analysis and therapy, that which is in the unconscious is brought into the conscious mind, where it can be addressed. Modern psychology often deals with behavior, but yoga science goes to the very core of the soul, from where springs mind and its modifications. Unless you know your own *sva-rupa*, your own real Self, you cannot have perfect control over your mind and its modifications.

NOW, Then, and Therefore
Yoga DISCIPLINE is Being Expounded

Now, then, and therefore yoga discipline is being expounded. *Atha yoganushasanam.* The first word that has been used is *now.* Nowhere else has this word been used in quite the way it is used here. *Now* is very important. *Now* means, "Now, then, and therefore." This means that there are preliminaries before you practice yoga science. The word *now* indicates that you have already completed the preliminaries. *Now* you want to attain more; you want to learn more; you want to understand more; you want to practice more.

When a teacher says, "*Now* do this," it means you have done something previously and you are ready to do something else *now.* A student should first be prepared and then choose the path of attainment. The first sutra explains indirectly, in a very subtle way, the role of the student. Yoga is a discipline and those who want to discipline themselves, who understand the importance of this discipline, should prepare themselves to learn, study, and practice yoga with mind, action, and speech. The qualification of a student is to prepare himself or herself not only to study and memorize the sutras, but also to practice.

Patanjali studied the mind on all levels and he describes several varieties of students: some are prepared, some are preparing, some are not at all prepared, and some are totally confused. These are not fit enough for preparation, so they are out of the question. Patanjali has put all levels of mind into five categories: *kshipta, vikshipta, mudha, ekagra,* and *niruddha. Kshipta* is a completely distracted mind. *Vikshipta* applies to those who have no control over their mind. They do not have a concentrated mind, but if they make effort, they can learn. Sometimes they understand and sometimes they do not understand because of their lack of attention. Their minds are not yet properly trained, but they are capable of being trained and accepted. That mind which remains in a state of stupor is called *mudha. Ekagra* refers to those who have a concentrated mind and can concentrate well. *Niruddha* describes those whose mind is completely under their control. They have trained their mind perfectly and can use it as they wish.

It is easy for a competent teacher to assess the mental condition of the student. When the student comes, the teacher can know what the problem is by the way the student walks. The teacher should know what type of mind the student has, whether the student is capable of studying this science or not, and if he is prepared. When the student comes, the teacher puts him in one of the categories. Has he got vikshipta mind? Is he mudha? Has he got ekagra or one-pointed mind? Has he got a completely controlled mind — niruddha? On this basis, the teacher immediately knows how to approach the student. This is like giving a prescription to a patient. If the teacher is wise and understands, he knows this.

When you are prepared, when you have completed the preliminaries, then the teacher tells you to do something else. The preliminaries are not described here. What the teacher said before *now*, only the student and teacher know. To study and practice and apply the sutras in your daily life, you have to prepare yourself. *Now* means you are prepared to study the sutras, to practice the sutras. *Now* you come to me. The word *now* indicates that you are fully prepared and it is a good time for you to start the next step. *Now* it is good that you are becoming aware of Reality. It is good that you want to know more. Whatever you have done so far is accepted. *Now*, here begins the exposition of yoga science. That has not been done yet. So far you have not learned it.

So the teacher says, "Now." You use this word from morning until evening but you do not understand what it means. Anyone who does not meditate cannot understand the word *now*. When you start examining your mind, you discover that mind is conditioned by three things—time, space, and causation. Time is a filter. Anything that happens goes through the filter of time. Today you may be sad and very worried and you may even be thinking of committing suicide. The next day, if I ask you if you are going to commit suicide, you will say no. If you give yourself time, later you will find that you do not feel that thing so much. The mind is conditioned by past, present, and future. The mind functions on the experiences of the past, or, on the basis of those experiences, on the imaginations of the future. Either you brood on the past, or you think of the future, but where is *now*? *Now* is missing. You do not know how to live here and *now*. What is the best period of a person's life? It is not that which you have spent already or the aspect of time you are going to utilize in the future. It is *now*. Utilize the best period of your life today and *now*. Can you really explain where that *now* is? You can spell the word, but you can never taste it. The moment you talk of *now*, it slips to the valley of the past. When you say *now*, then there is no *now*. It is not there. How many of you enjoy *now*? You plan for your vacation next year, you plan for going out for dinner and dancing, but what happens *now*? You know the word, you know the meaning, but you do not know how to enjoy it. Your mind either goes into the grooves of past experiences or future imagination. It has never realized *now*. But if there is no *now*, then where is the link between past and future? In your daily life you postpone your happiness because you do not know how to be in the present. *Now* is missing in your life. If you can get freedom from past experiences and you can stop your mind from imagining the future, you will enjoy *now*. If you learn how to make your mind free from time, you will be beyond all this. Fortunate are those who meditate and live in the *now*. Through meditation you can enjoy *now*. It is in *now* that there is enjoyment, or part of eternity. The moment you come to know *now* you will know past, present, and future; you will be free.

The other conditions of mind are space and causation. If I hold up my hand and show you two separate fingers, what is the "cause" of these two fingers? The hand is the cause that creates the awareness of fingers. When I hold my fingers apart, they seem separate. If the hand were not there, then it would not create the space between the two fingers. This is called causation—that which creates effect. If I hold the two fingers together, there is no space between them and there will be no sense of time. Then it is one with causation. My fingers are still part of one whole. Mind can be freed from these three conditionings. So many thoughts come and you call it the thinking process. There is a space between two thoughts. But if there is no space between two thoughts, then what will happen to time? Time will not exist. If there is only one thought, what will be the condition of space? There will be no space at all. Time and space are variations of the same thing. If there is only one thought in the mind, then time cannot affect the mind. One cannot attain the highest state of samadhi without gaining freedom from the conditionings of the mind. When mind can fathom the boundaries of time, then mind can realize the subtler levels of consciousness and transform itself. Then, it can lead you to a state of peace, happiness, and joy. If mind is free from imagination — I am not talking about creative imagination — and from the memories of the past, then mind can be brought to a state of *now*. If you learn to train your mind to be here and *now*, you will know everything. There is nothing to be known beyond that. *Now* is part of eternity. When a teacher teaches you, first learn how to be here and *now*, for you have completed the preliminaries. *Now*, learn to understand the word *now*.

Patanjali leads you to an inward journey. His first lesson is, *You have to discipline yourself. Now, then, therefore, go aspire.* Before you study yoga science, you should be fully prepared, because it requires discipline.

Yoga is a Science that Deals with Body, Breath, Mind, Soul, and Ultimately, the Universe Itself

What does yoga science mean to you? When people talk about yoga they often think it has something to do with the physical being only. Yoga is a science that deals with body, breath, mind, soul, and ultimately, the universe itself. It is both practical and theoretical.

Patanjali is not trying to teach any particular religion to you. Yoga is not a new religion, nor does it condemn any religion. Yoga does not teach that if you are Jewish, you should become Catholic, or if you are Catholic, you should become Hindu, or if you are Hindu, you should become Buddhist. All the great religions have come from one source. Religions tell people what to do and what not to do, and provide a set of rules or commandments that are not fully satisfying. Yoga science does not tell you what to do and what not to do, but teaches you how to be. Yoga science is a science of life that helps you to know the known and unknown parts of life, that helps you to liberate yourself from pains and miseries, and that helps you to attain that state which is free from pains and miseries.

How can someone living in the world practice yoga science? If you understand the fundamental principles of yoga science and why yoga science should be practiced, it will become easy for you to practice. First you have to decide to search. You have to feel the necessity of finding yourself. *Yes, I want to know myself. Something is missing, something I could not receive from my church, from my religion.* Millions of people, both in the East and in the West, are searching for Truth and Self-realization — or as the religionists put it, God. You may go to church or temple or synagogues, but the questioning mind is still there. Sometimes orthodox religions do not satisfy your needs, so you question life. When your mind questions, it means you are not fully satisfied. Life is a question in front of you. You want to know something more, but you are using this little mind, which is like a yardstick, to measure the vast universe and its mysteries. You do not understand your religion because you do not understand yourself. The highest of all books is the book of life. Unless you open the book of life, you will not understand the teachings of the scriptures. The scriptures say what to do and what not to do, but you have to learn how to be. All the gates to higher knowledge will be opened to you once you understand yourself. Patanjali offers something to such seekers. Patanjali says the source of knowledge is within you. The world and external knowledge can only inform you and inspire you. To evolve does not mean going toward the external world. Evolution means going back to the source. If you put ten covers around a light, what will happen to the light? The light will be as it is, but it will appear dim to you. You will not be able to see it. If you remove the covers, you will see it clearly. You can compare yourself with the light. Before you go to the source of knowledge within, you have to go through many barriers.

Yoga science does not offer any new religion; it offers a methodology. Through yoga science you can understand yourself better on all levels, including your physical well-being, your actions, thought process, emotions, and desires. You will also understand how you are related to the world, and how to lead a successful life in the world. Yoga science creates a bridge between the internal and external conditions of life. Yoga is a way of improving yourself, a way of understanding your internal states. Whosoever you are, you have all the potentials within you. Are you aware of this? If you are aware of this, do you know how to use them? Patanjali encourages us to be aware of the potentials that we have and to learn how to use them. This practical science says to explore more and more.

The word *yoga* means "unification, to unite with." You have to unite yourself with the whole. At present you are an individual and you are experiencing miseries. The cause of misery, according to Patanjali, is ignorance. Ignorance is self-created. You can be free from that misery because it has been created by you. It's as if you constantly slap your face and then say, *God help me.* It's as though you blindfold yourself and then say, *O Lord of light, of life, and love, give me light.* This prayer is in vain.

DISCIPLINE Means Self-Commitment

You have to light your own lamp. No one will give you salvation. I am talking of enlightenment. All individuals have the responsibility to enlighten themselves. Do not think you cannot do it. You have that spark. You are fully equipped. You simply need to discipline yourself. Discipline is not a prison. It simply means practice.

Patanjali says that you have the capacity to unfold yourself and lead yourself to a state of tranquility. Then you will understand things as they are. Otherwise, you create darkness for yourself and you are not able to see things clearly. The human mind remains clouded because the external world does not provide correct data. In the external world everything is fleeting. The moment you want to study something in the external world, that thing changes its name and form and you cannot study it. First, you will have to remove the clouds of ignorance from your mind. When you have clarity of mind, then you can study things as they are, and there will be no confusion.

Thus, when Patanjali says, *Atha yoganush-asanam*, he means that if you really want to unfold yourself, you first should learn to discipline yourself. People are afraid of the word *discipline*. Discipline is

not a punishment. You will enjoy it once you know it.
Discipline means self-commitment. When you commit
yourself to your progress, then slowly you will find
that the light is within you. These external lights —
the sun, moon, stars, and electric lights — are superficial
lights. The Upanishads say again and again, *hiran-
mayena patrena satyasyapihitam mukham, tat tvam
pushann apavrinu satya dharmaya drishtaye.* (Ishopanishad 15). "The face of Truth is hidden by the
golden disc. Oh Lord, help me so that I can see the
Truth within." You keep trying to find Truth in the
external world, but it is not there. Those who have
found Truth within themselves can express that same
Truth in the external world, and they are considered
to be great people.

The discipline you need to learn this science, to
follow the path for the inward journey, is not the
discipline that you already have. You have to
understand this subtle point. You had to have
discipline in the colleges and universities to study
things in the external world and to verify things in
the external world. Learning in the external world is
entirely different from yoga discipline. In the external
world you move. However, when you want to go to
the deeper levels of your being, stillness is important.
In all other journeys you have to move. In this journey
you do not have to move at all. The Bible says, "Be
still and know that I am God." It is a simple formula,
but very difficult to apply. From your childhood
onward you are taught to move. Nobody teaches you
how to be still. You have to learn not to move.
Anushasanam, the discipline that you have to follow,
you have not yet learned. Since it is a completely new
undertaking, it seems difficult. To learn yoga science,
which leads you to the highest rungs of life, which

takes you to the summum bonum of life, which leads
you to the kingdom of wisdom, peace, and bliss, and
which leads you to freedom from all pains and
miseries, you first have to discipline yourself. In
modern education there is enough knowledge, enough
books, and enough freedom, but there is no training
program for discipline. No one tells you how to study
yourself or how to practice. Patanjali says this is not
the way. That knowledge which you consider to be
knowledge is not fruitful or helpful. First, learn to
discipline yourself. At any age, at any time, you can
discipline yourself. It is not too late. You have to
discipline yourself. Discipline is real learning. Learn
to say *no* to yourself. Listen to that part of mind that
tells you *no*. If you really want to practice, for some
time don't listen to that part of mind that says *yes*. If
you understand *no* well, you will understand *yes*
easily. When you want to steal something, mind says,
Don't. Another part of mind says, *Oh, yes. Come on,
do it. You'll enjoy it. You'll like it. You should have it.*
Don't listen to the *yes*. Listen to *no* first. Tell yourself
you're not going to do that. You have to understand
the impact of *no* and learn to use it with yourself and
not with others. Never use the word *no* with others,
with those with whom you live, or with those whom
you love. Learn to use that *no* for yourself. This will
give you strength. Discipline should not be forced by
teachers or by others. Patanjali says the whole
foundation of samadhi is anushasanam. You have to
understand the word *anushasanam* in a practical way.
Discipline means to regulate yourself on three levels:
mind, action, and speech. Determine that from today
you will begin to discipline yourself. It is a simple thing.
Do not make big plans or too many rigid rules for
yourself. Start with small things: *I will wake up at four-
thirty.* One simple rule. *After that, I will go to finish my*

ablutions and do my exercise. Exactly at five-thirty I will sit down in meditation. Discipline yourself. If you do not have the zeal, vigor, and determination to discipline yourself, you cannot follow the path. When you have decided something, you need determination to act according to your decision. If you lack determination, you will not be successful, even though you have decided. If you have decided that you will practice yoga, that decision must be supported by determination. *Yes. I will practice it every day. The day I don't practice, I will not eat.* The next day you will say, *I have to practice because I have to eat.*

When a student comes to a teacher he wants to see a miracle. You yourself are a miracle. How did Christ change water into wine? Only a perfect yoga master could do that. Do you know what Christ did? There was an essay contest on this topic among the writers of Britain when I was studying in Europe. One person answered the question in one line and he won the prize. The line was, "When the master looked upon the beloved, she blushed." When Christ looked at the water, the water changed its color. Anything around you is subject to change according to the way you look at it. The day you understand this principle your entire environment can be changed if you are really disciplined. Do not blame nature, God, or others. Ninety-nine percent of your problems are self-created. You know it, though you do not accept it.

You say you cannot get enlightened, you can never see God. You have a desire to see God, yet you have no concept or understanding of what God is, so nothing is going to happen. You are searching for enlightenment in the external world, but that is not the way. Are you prepared for the journey from the grossest to the subtlest aspect of your being? Are you competent enough to discipline yourself on all levels? Can you practice? Are you prepared to know life within and without? If you are, come along. How will you do it? *Now, yoga science is being expounded.* What is that exposition? How can you create a bridge between the external and the internal? How can you understand all the mysteries of life here and hereafter? How can you understand your relationship with the universe? How can you understand the purpose of your life? All this will be explained, but first you should understand mind and its modifications.

Having CONTROL Over MIND AND ITS MODIFICATIONS, You Attain the Highest State of Wisdom, SAMADHI

The second sutra explains the aim of the entire yoga psychology. *Yogash chitta-vritti-nirodhah.* There are two meanings for this. By applying the yogic methods that are being explained to you by your teacher, you can have control over mind and its modifications, and thus attain samadhi, the highest state of wisdom; this is one meaning. Having control over mind and its modifications is called yoga; this is the second meaning.

The word *yoga* has many connotations, but here it means "samadhi." The word *yoga* comes from the root *yuj*, and it means "to unite, to join." When prana and apana are joined, that is called yoga. When an individual soul is united with the cosmic soul, that is called yoga. When one attains samadhi, that is also called yoga. The aim and object of yoga is to attain the highest of all states—samadhi. Patanjali is not talking about seeing God; whether or not God exists is not the point of Patanjali. He says, "Oh man, you have to know yourself on all levels." First, you have to understand yourself on all levels, and then you can understand the Self of all, the Absolute Self, that is called Absolute Truth.

The central theme of the yoga sutras is samadhi, that which in Sanskrit is called *samahitam*. The Upanishads beautifully explain it: *yada panca-vatishthante jnanani manasa saha, buddhish cha na vicheshthate tam ahuh paramam gatim* (Kathopanishad 6.10). The highest of all states is that state of tranquility that is never disturbed, no matter what happens, in all conditions of life. There is a state of tranquility in which your mind becomes balanced, and that state of tranquility leads you to a fourth dimension, *turiya*, or samadhi, the super-conscious state. You are aware of only three states at present — the states of waking, dreaming, and sleeping. All human beings are aware of these three states, but only a fortunate few, the great sages or yogis who tread the internal path, are aware of the fourth state, the highest state of tranquility, called samadhi.

Samadhi is beyond all joys. Joys last only for some time, and then again the darkness and sadness come. Samadhi is constant. There is no question of any sadness, sorrow, or misery. By attaining that state you come in touch with the source of knowledge and infinite love within, the library of intuitive knowledge. The fourth state is free from all problems whatsoever — worldly, spiritual, or divine. All conflicts within and without are resolved. Nothing in the world can disturb you.

Your mind is always going through *samkalpa* and *vikalpa*, arguing for and against, brooding on something all the time. Can you imagine a state that is free from all questions and argumentation? When all your problems and questions are resolved, in which language will you think? If your mind has attained a state that is free from all conflicts, what is the condition of your mind? If there is no question in your mind, how can your mind continue the usual thinking process? In which language will you think when you have nothing to think, when you have no questions at all? What will your mind do then? The human mind functions within a certain field. You will go beyond that. There is nothing in the unconscious that you have not seen before. Your mind works only within the boundaries of the field of whatever you have previously heard, seen, thought of, or imagined. This is the field of the phenomenal world. Patanjali says you can cross that field. Your mind wanders within a boundary of its own, but it can go beyond. You are not aware of that. There is a way of training your mind and all the various faculties of your mind so that you can go beyond. There are many other fields where mind gets freedom from all these forms, and remains in a state of joy and happiness. *Beyond* means the transpersonal field. The field of your personal mind is small. When you know that this field is not able to help you, then you cross to the transpersonal field. Then you will find that you receive help, and you can help yourself in a better way. Self-confidence is important, but it is also essential to take help from the transpersonal mind. You will cross the mire of delusion and go to the kingdom of spirituality, the kingdom of light, where pains and miseries will not affect you, and you will be in a state of constant joy or bliss. A human being can do that.

There are five "vehicles" described by yoga science. We have described these vehicles in detail in the book, *Yoga and Psychotherapy*.[1] The physical body is the grossest vehicle. The second is the vital force or

[1]Swami Rama, Rudolph Ballentine, M.D., Swami Ajaya, Ph.D. *Yoga and Psychotherapy*. Honesdale, Pennsylvania. Himalayan Institute Press, 1976.

pranic sheath—the sheath of prana or energy that you inhale and exhale with the breath. The third is the mental sheath. The fourth is the sheath of your personal knowledge, and the fifth is the sheath of bliss. The fifth sheath is blissful because it is very close to the center of consciousness; it is the mirror of the center of consciousness. It can be called the conscience within.

Patanjali does not begin discussing the body or the breath first. He directly goes to mind and its modifications. Even if you train your body, and apply all your resources to train your body, still you will never know Truth. First, learn to understand your mind and purify your mind in an orderly way. You can do it. One who has understood the mind has understood everything. You do not have to worry in order to understand God; you do not have to worry to understand the center of consciousness. It is already there, even if you do not believe it is there. It is your mind that makes a difference. Patanjali says you have something permanent with you that is called "the monkey mind." That monkey mind always gets in your way and creates barriers for you. One day it helps you to understand something, and then the next day you undo the same thing. One moment you think you have known something; after half an hour, the same mind will say you have not known anything. Sometimes you think you are going toward insanity; sometimes you think you are doing very well. That monkey mind comes between you and realization. It is all mind. *Mana eva manushyanam karanam bandha-mokshayoh.* It is mind that creates a barrier for you, but mind can also help you in gaining emancipation or liberation. Mind is an obstacle for the ignorant, and a means for the wise. The same mind that is considered to be an obstacle can be a useful tool provided you know your mind.

If you put five, six, seven, or eight shades on a table lamp, you will find the light seems very dim. If you go on removing the shades, finally you will find the light. The limitations of the mind are exactly like those shades. There are various levels of mind to penetrate before reaching the kingdom of the soul — personal mind, transpersonal mind, inner mind, collective mind, and cosmic mind. When you go to the center of consciousness, you will not find mind there. You will only find consciousness itself. Consciousness is different from mind. Mind is an instrument that has various functions. How does your mind function and from where does it receive power and energy? Mind functions because of the power called consciousness. Mind is the instrument; consciousness is the power. There is a center of consciousness beyond mind called your individual soul. The power that mind is using for thinking, listening, understanding, and judging comes from the soul. Mind has its limitations. In *Ishopanishad* it is written, *tadejati tan naijati tad dure tad vantike, tad antarasya sarvasya tad u sarvasyasya bahyatah* (Ishopanishad 5). It is a description for Atman or the soul. There is no movement, yet Atman runs faster than the mind. It means if Atman is everywhere, where can you run? Mind cannot run faster than the soul because the soul is everywhere. Mind is only an instrument that can fathom a very small part of the power of the soul or the center of consciousness. Mind receives energy from the center of consciousness. Consciousness is singular in number, but there are many levels of consciousness. There are also various levels of enlightenment and various levels of ignorance. If you become aware of the levels of ignorance before treading the path of enlightenment, you can easily tread the path.

I want to teach you about mind first, and then about body and soul. In English, the word *man* is actually from a Sanskrit word, *manas*, which means mind. *Man* should be pronounced as *mun*, not *man*. "Oh man, you are a thinking being. You are not only a physical being and a breathing being like the animals; you are also a thinking being. The capacity to think is not found in the other kingdoms. That is why I call you man."

Patanjali directly deals with the mind and its modifications. First of all, you should be aware that you are a thinking being. It is your nature to think. He is not talking about something abstract or over your head or about the soul. Patanjali goes directly to the point, which is *chitta*, the thinking self. Though chitta is also translated as mind, Patanjali is not talking about what modern psychology calls mind, but about something far more comprehensive. He is talking about the totality of all mental functioning. Chitta is the field in which the rest of the mind functions. All aspects of chitta are modifications.

Patanjali makes you aware of your mind first, because it is mind, both conscious and unconscious, its various aspects and functions, and all its *vrittis* or modifications that create a wall between you and Reality. Mind comes in the way and creates many problems, but you should remember that the mind is yours. You do not belong to your mind. You can control your mind provided you understand it. Controlling the mind does not mean stopping the thought process. Control of the mind means using it properly, and knowing the method of using the forces of the mind.

You know only a small part of your mind, the conscious mind. You use the conscious mind only during the waking state. Though the conscious mind is very important, it is only a small part of the totality of the mind. Most of the time you are not conscious of the things around you and you are not conscious of the duties you are performing. What you call the conscious mind is not subject to control. Anybody who attempts to control the conscious mind is committing a serious mistake and wasting time and energy. The training that you receive from your homes and environments, from your educational systems, from your colleges and universities, deals only with the conscious mind and the waking state. The educational systems all over the world teach you to cultivate only the conscious mind, but the waking state is not your total life. You have such a vast reservoir, an infinite library within you, but your education does not help you in knowing and having control over the totality of mind. That is why you are confused.

First, you should try to understand the limitations of the conscious mind. The study of the conscious mind is very interesting. The objective mind uses the five cognitive senses. Cognition takes place because of the objective mind. Even during the waking state you are not properly utilizing the conscious mind. When you do not know how to use your conscious mind, you lose the capacity of being here and now in the present. You remain either in the grooves of the past or in the grooves of future imagination; you do not know how to use the present. This is not reality: the past has gone and the future is not here. You are not enjoying life as you should. To live here and now first you have to understand the functioning of the conscious or objective mind, which is constantly receiving sensations from the external world.

You have not explored most of your mental states. A vast part of your mind remains unknown and uncultivated. No one teaches you about the unconscious mind. When you are not in the waking state, then you are in the sleeping state or the dreaming state. When you are in the waking state, you do not know what happens to the parts of your mind that go to the dreaming state or sleeping state. What happens in your dreaming and sleeping states? You wake up either when you are fully rested, or when you have been disturbed. Who tells you that now you have had enough rest, you have slept for a long time, and should wake up? Most people cannot voluntarily go to rest and say that they will sleep for half an hour, but there is a technique like that. You do not know that technique. Just tell yourself that no matter what happens, from two to four you have to sleep because you have to work. If you learn the secrets of sleep, no one in the world can disturb you, no matter how many drums they beat or how much noise they make. You have no conscious control over your dreams. Why are you not taught to dream the way you want? Why are you not taught to sleep the way you want? How do you train that part of mind that dreams and that part that goes to sleep? What does sleep mean to you? Do you understand the anatomy of sleep? Do you know there is a fourth state called turiya? All these questions are omitted because there are no scientific instruments to test and verify. You do not know how to train the totality of the mind and the different functions of the mind. A vast part of the mind remains buried in the unknown. You have not yet explored the greatest part of your mental states. Even if you have explored them somewhat, you haven't got the means to inspect them. You are only using the objective mind — the conscious mind and the senses together. Even if you know the method, the conscious mind and the ten senses are not sufficient to inspect the whole mind. You cannot learn the technique of knowing the whole mind if you are restricted to the senses. You will have to go to another dimension. The conscious mind is not an instrument for knowing the totality of your mind. Unless you change the conscious mind, it is not possible for you to study the unconscious mind. You know only a covering called body and senses and conscious mind. If you only know your garment and do not know yourself, what will happen to you? You are ignoring the real you that is within — the unconscious mind and the soul. One who has not gone inside is lost outside.

You have no control over your mind. You see things the way you do because you use only a small part of your mind. If you awaken your total mind, you will see things as they are. When you know the whole mind, then the part that you use in your daily life will easily come under your control. Not only can you bring the conscious mind that you use during the waking state under your control, but also the part of mind that functions only during the dreaming state, or the part of mind that creates a state of deep sleep for you. You can control the totality of your mind and become more dynamic and more powerful. The values of things change when you understand them. If you are sitting in front of a window, you will see a very small part of the horizon. If you go outside, you will see a larger horizon. But if you go to the top of the roof, you will see the whole horizon clearly. When you understand the totality of your mind, there will be no problem at all. At present you are seeing things with small eyes. If you are able to make your whole being an eye, everything will definitely look different.

When you learn to fathom the different states of mind one after another—the waking, dreaming, and sleeping states—you can then attain the fourth state, the superconscious state of your mind. You can attain that state during the waking state. Actually the fourth state is the expansion of your conscious mind. Just as mind functions on conscious and unconscious levels, mind also works on a higher level called the superconscious level. If you do not achieve the superconscious level, how can you verify the knowledge gained from the conscious mind? Everyone lives to attain the superconscious state. Everyone lives with the hope of attaining happiness—if not today, then tomorrow, or the day after tomorrow. We all have one and the same aim, and that aim is to attain happiness. Sometimes people experiment on the physical level and they experience some joy, but it does not last for a long time. *Vishayananda*, the bliss experienced in physical unity, is only momentary. It gives you hope that this small moment of happiness can be expanded, and that *paramananda*, the highest bliss, the highest of joys, can be realized and attained in this lifetime. It is not impossible. When you understand the primary necessity, the goal of life, you will become aware of Reality. Try to understand the discipline and the knowledge that are being expounded, and directly apply them to the mind.

You are a Projection of That Which You Call MIND

Patanjali dived into the deeper realms of his being and discovered the various functions of the mind. Just as you have four external limbs — two lower extremities and two upper extremities — so your *antah-karana* (your inner being) also has four limbs. *Antah* means, "inside," and *karana* means, "that which functions." That which functions inside is the real person; that which functions outside is only a projection of the real person. You are a projection of that which you call mind. The whole of the body is in the mind, but the whole of the mind is not in the body. Therefore, the body will follow the mind; mind does not follow body. Mind is not a projection of body, but body is a projection of mind.

You have four separate functions or faculties of your mind that are modifications: *ahamkara* (ego), *manas* (sensory or lower mind), *buddhi* (intellect), and *chitta* (the unconscious reservoir or storehouse of all impressions). These faculties create obstacles for you and you are searching for enlightenment in the external world. That is not the way. If you do not understand these four distinct functions of mind, you cannot understand the more internal states. Manas remains busy in sorting out and in understanding the things going on in the external world. Buddhi is that which judges, discriminates, and decides what to do and what not to do. Another function of mind, the ahamkara, remains busy in understanding and becoming aware of the self in a limited way. The word *chitta* is used here as a function of the mind. In this smaller context, chitta, the storehouse of impressions, represents the "unconscious" of modern psychology. Thought waves arise from chitta and surface in the sensory-motor mind, manas. All this is going on in the workshop called body. Mind is the manager of this busy workshop. Mind has many assistants and hardly recognizes the real boss. That is why mind completely takes over and uses the whole body.

Mind assumes many forms. Ahamkara, or ego, is one of these. Ego creates great mires of delusion. Ego makes you forget the Reality. Ego is that which separates you from the whole, which makes you small, and contracts your personality. That which makes you an individual and does not allow you to expand yourself to become the cosmic Self is your ego. The ego is a barrier that stands between you and the Reality. It never wants to allow you to know the Reality because it has cheated the Reality. It is also ego that makes you think you are so small and you are so bad. The ego misuses all the human resources. It is because of ego that you are not aware of the divine within and you have not attained another state of wisdom.

It is very important to understand the role manas plays in your life. Manas has employed ten agencies — the *indriyas* (ten senses) — because manas has a powerful job. Manas is responsible for importing and exporting information. When manas wants to work in the external world, it uses these ten agencies — the *karmendriya* (the five gross senses) and the *jyanendriya* (the five subtle senses). The manager is always busy giving work to these ten messengers.

The five gross senses are: the capacity to speak, to work with your hands, to move with your feet, and to procreate and to eliminate — the two front and rear gates. The subtle senses are five distinct channels for the mind to flow toward the objects of the external world — the capacities to see, hear, touch, smell, and taste. These are more active and swifter than the gross senses. If I want to come to you, it will take some time. If I think of you, you are there immediately through the sense of sight. The creator of the arrangement of nature is wonderful.

When the senses contact matter, you experience one of three types of sensations. One is painful, another is pleasant, and the other is neither painful nor pleasant. When you go from your home to your office you see many trees. That sensation gives you neither pain nor pleasure. When you see a friend and you smile, that pleases you. If you see someone who annoys you every day, that gives you pain. The contact of the senses with the objects of the world brings sensations that are pleasurable, painful, or neither pleasurable nor painful.

The senses are the greatest source of distraction for your mind. The moment you wake up in the morning your conscious mind starts using your senses. It appears that the senses are contacting the objects of the world, but actually it is the mind that is doing the contacting. The ten senses are totally dependent on the mind. The moment your mind becomes active, the ten senses become active. With the help of the senses, manas receives sensations. When you see something, that sight affects you. When you hear something, that sound affects you. When you smell something, that odor affects you. When you taste something, that taste affects you. When you touch something, that sensation affects you. You receive sensations constantly. These sensations are filtered by the conscious mind. If I look at you, the impression of you is taken by my optic nerve to my brain, then to the conscious mind, and finally to the unconscious mind, where it settles. The brain is not the mind; the brain is the seat of the mind. The mind is like electricity, the brain is like a bulb, and the nervous system is like the network of wires. Mind works through the nervous system. When you understand this relationship then you can learn how to deal with them in a coordinated way. Those impressions are transmitted by the various sensory organs to the brain, and then are stored in chitta, the unconscious. All things going through the conscious mind finally settle down in the unconscious. The conscious mind gives importance or meaning to the sensations that you receive according to your interests. If you are looking at me but your mind is somewhere else, you will not understand what I am saying. You will not even know how I am moving, though your eyes and ears are wide open and you are sitting right next to me. You cannot understand me, yet you are still recording a sensation and the impressions will go to your unconscious mind. What if I stop looking at you and I look at something else? When I look at you again, why do I remember you? I remember that I have seen you before because your impression is already there in the unconscious. Immediately the unconscious comes forward to the conscious mind and says, *I have seen this person before.* That is how you know, and know that you know — with the help of the vast reservoir within you, the unconscious mind.

Manas uses the senses to go out to the objects of the world. Manas imports and exports through the ten senses, but it has no power to import and export whatever it wants. Manas is called the doubtful faculty of your mind. Before you do something, first manas says, *Shall I do it or not?* That is why mind is called *samkalpa-vikalpatmakam mana.* Manas has no power to decide. Sometimes you want to decide, but you wait. You want to see; you want to judge; you want to understand. *Shall I read now? Oh, it is too late. I should go there.* The decision time comes. *But how am I going to write my paper?* You can go through this argumentation for a long time. Opposing sensations or opposing thought patterns can torment you. A thought comes that you should study your book. Then another thought comes. *Don't study. It doesn't matter what happens. If I don't get 'B', I'll get 'C', so what?* Another opposing sensation comes. *Life is so long. I have many years to live. I can do it tomorrow.* You can learn to control those sensations that create obstacles in your daily life.

If you learn to control samkalpa and vikalpa, the opposing sensations will cease tormenting you. *Samkalpa* means "determination;" *vikalpa* means "lack of determination." Sometimes you want to do something, yet you do not want to do it. You are continuously experiencing conflict. *Shall I do it, or shall I not do it?* Conflicts arise in your mind because you do not know how to decide things on time. The nature of manas is to argue and to pose questions, but it has no power to decide, to judge, or to discriminate. These are the functions of the faculty called buddhi. Manas, the doubtful part of your mind, puts both sides before buddhi, the decisive faculty, and immediately buddhi makes a decision. *If you study, you will be able to write a good paper. But you are tired so you should not study.*

Buddhi has the very important post of financial advisor. Buddhi checks manas. It is the accountant of the factory, the CPA, which says, *You do not have that much capacity. Do not do that. Do not export too much. Do not import too much. We do not have that much money.* You need to train your buddhi, which discriminates, judges, and decides, so that your mind can import and export according to your capacity. If you go beyond your capacity, the firm will fail. Is your buddhi prepared and sharpened enough to teach manas? Is manas listening to your buddhi? When your mind brings something before you to do, you first have to decide whether you should do it or not. Buddhi helps you to discriminate between what should be accepted and what should be rejected. This is going on all the time.

Some people can decide things accurately by recalling their past memories, by creative imagination. Immediately they come to a certain conclusion and they are correct. Others cannot decide for a long time. They are afraid to decide because they are afraid of failure. They think, *If I do not achieve, what will happen? It is urgent that I decide this thing on time, but I never learned to do that. I was afraid to decide some things so I never heard the voice of my decisive faculty. I will not believe it.* Many times this happens.

Some people train their minds only to argue and they can never come to conclusions. They do not allow the decisive faculty to help them. Many people can think but cannot make decisions. They are great thinkers and great worriers but they are not warriors. Those who have not trained all the functions of mind are completely controlled by their tendencies and they cannot decide things on time. When something important comes, you have to decide immediately. If you have not trained your buddhi, then you will think, *Shall I jump or shall I go this way? Shall I jump or shall I go that way?* By that time the bus will have departed. If you take two years' time to decide what you need to decide today, you will miss the bus and you will repent your whole life. If you learn to decide things on time, you will never miss the bus in life.

Even if you know far more than others know, you may still be a failure if you do not decide things on time. Today's intellectuals have a serious problem. They sharpen only one side of the intellect, and they do not know how to decide. They have not sharpened another aspect of the same buddhi that deals with decisiveness, discrimination, and judging. The secret lies in having a one-pointed mind. You must train your intellect to become one-pointed. When your intellect is sharpened it has decisive power and it does not allow you to create conflict. Conflict within and without is the cause of all miseries. Without the faculty of discrimination you will remain in a state of conflict. If you learn to decide things on time, there will be no conflict. Conflict means you could not make a decision in time. The lack of decision leads to more conflict, and then conflict becomes the source of pain. Learn to strengthen your decisive faculty within.

All human beings have an inborn tendency to experience for themselves. A child who is repeatedly warned not to go toward the fire will go to the fire anyway, even though he loves you and wants to listen to you. If you do not allow him to go to the fire, he will go when you are not there and experience it for himself. When you talk of self-experience, you are cheating yourself. All day you have many experiences, but there are few experiences in life that guide you. You have experiences the whole day, but still you do not have confidence in yourself. Why are you not fully confident that if you do a certain thing, it will help you? You do not have confidence because the experience has not come through the right source. You have millions of experiences in your lifetime, but how many of your experiences help you in daily life? Experience which does not guide you is not really right experience. Experience cannot be repeated confidently by you if you do not have dynamic will. You do not think, *I will do this and I will reap this result,* because your experience has not come through the right source. Have you ever seen anybody drinking the best wine in a paper cup? Have you ever seen milk flowing through a gutter? The purest and highest consciousness also needs the right channeling. Right experience is the right channel for the knowledge that you use in the external world. If you learn how to decide things on time, then you will have direct experience. Direct experience alone can guide you.

You have the capacity and the potential to train the buddhi. Once you start training the buddhi, you will not waste time in judging, deciding, or doing things as you should. You will have clarity of mind, clarity of intellect. Your intellect will immediately make decisions and you will receive the fruits according to your desires. That means doing things skillfully. When you learn to do your actions skillfully, the next step is to do them selflessly — to dedicate the fruits of your actions to others. The result is that you will become great yogis in the world. If you gain freedom from the misery that you have now, how can you be sure that in the future there will be no misery? Patanjali says you can prevent and control future misery by understanding the power of the intellect, that part of mind that decides and judges. Buddhi is that particular faculty that helps you to know something. When you have sharpened it properly, when you have not allowed it to remain dull, it can judge and decide. Then your penetrative nature will help you to understand that which is real and that which is not real. *Viveka*, or knowledge, is the product of a sharpened buddhi.

The faculty of discrimination or intellect can help you to sort out the things of your conscious mind, but a time comes when your faculty of discrimination cannot help you. It has no power to go to your unconscious mind to help you. This is very important. You should allow your intellect to sort out the things that the unconscious mind brings forward to your conscious mind, or you will not be successful.

There are many levels of chitta, the reservoir of your unconscious mind. The unconscious mind is a storehouse for all the impressions you have been storing. As a river cannot flow without a bed, there also has to be a bed for the flow of thoughts. The unconscious mind is actually part of the conscious mind. You do not have conscious and unconscious dreams, or conscious and unconscious sleep. What you call the unconscious is really a part of – another level of – the conscious mind. But if it is a level of the conscious mind, then why are you not aware of it? You are not even aware of the conscious mind because you do not study and train it.

The mind can be compared to an iceberg. The largest part of that iceberg remains under water, while only a small part is visible above the water. You are trying to analyze only the conscious mind, that little part which is seen outside. The counterpart is the latent part — that which you are not aware of, which you do not know. That which is submerged, that which is there but not visible, is the unconscious. Even if you can control the conscious mind, at times you will find the hidden part of the iceberg rising to the surface, and then you think, *I never knew that about myself. I never knew that I could think like that, that I could do things like that.* Even if you work with yourself, sometimes the latent part suddenly comes and reveals itself. You should understand that your subtler self makes your personality. Your outer personality does not make your subtler self. The way you are at present is exactly the same way that you are in your latent condition. Your face will not appear beautiful in the mirror if you are ugly in your astral body. When dirty ice melts, the water will also be dirty. Become aware that you have to work with yourself. Otherwise, unknowingly, unconsciously, you will experience constant depression. Without understanding your unconscious, life remains a mystery. It poses a big, serious question for which the books have no answer.

The functioning of the unconscious mind has not yet been properly studied. All sensations go to the unconscious mind. There are several levels in the unconscious mind where you store impressions. All thought forms arise from the unconscious mind, though in a very subtle form. You know them when they come to the conscious level.

If you know how to disconnect from sensory contact, you will not receive fresh sensations. But what about those sensations you have already stored in the unconscious mind? There is always turmoil in the unconscious mind. If you have a conviction about certain things, and another sensation is received that is stronger than the previous conviction, the impression of the conviction that is stored in your mind will be affected by the new conviction. In this way silent turmoil and underground currents are going on in the ocean of mind called unconscious all the time. You are not aware that sometimes the unconscious mind simultaneously functions when you are using the conscious mind. Your mind is helping you and protecting you from the sensations that create emotions, and your unconscious mind is receiving something against which you are fighting mentally.

Unconscious suggestions are much more powerful than conscious suggestions. Suppose I have a good friend and someone comes and speaks against my friend again and again. My conscious mind does not accept what he is saying because I know my friend. After he is gone, my unconscious mind, which has accepted what he said, tells me that maybe it is true. My conscious mind has not accepted anything at all, but unconsciously I have accepted it. That is why the questioning comes. *It is possible that my friend must have done that. Why did he not tell me? I did not really know the nature of my friend. I am so sad.*

Even though you disagree consciously, you may accept someone's suggestions unconsciously. This is the case with the myth of ghosts. If someone says a ghost lives under that tree, I am not prepared to listen. My mind is very scientific, very argumentative, and very rational, and I am not prepared to accept this. By chance, one night while I am walking under that tree, I remember suddenly that someone said a ghost lives under that tree. This happens because unconsciously I have accepted the suggestion made by the other person. When you argue with someone, even though you stick to your own philosophy, the opponent affects your unconscious mind because the unconscious receives even that which is beyond agreement of your conscious mind.

After my parents died a woman looked after me during my childhood. She was not capable of controlling me. I was very naughty, running here and there, as children do. Trying to find a way to control me, she said, "Look, if you go over there, you will see a ghost and that ghost will pick you up."

I never believed her because I knew that she was definitely trying to control me. Still, I was very anxious to see the ghost, just out of curiosity. I was not afraid because I did not believe her. All the people around me were very nice to me and no one's name was "ghost." Consciously I did not accept her suggestion, but I accepted it unconsciously. When I visit that place today I still remember the story of the ghost. I have not forgotten it.

NIRODHAH Means to Cultivate, to Coordinate All the Aspects of Your Mind

When you understand the nature of your mind and its modifications, then you can try to understand the way of regulating your mind and having control over it. Your mind is like a lake. All the vrittis or modifications are waves in the lake of the mind. You cannot know what is in the unconscious mind because the conscious mind is very much disturbed. As long as there is turmoil in the lake of mind, you cannot see what is hidden beneath. If you cannot calm down even the conscious part of mind, how can you touch the whole of the unconscious, how can you dive deep into the unconscious?

The sutra says, *Yogash chitta-vritti-nirodhah.* Because of the confusion in language many writers have translated the word *nirodhah* as suppression or repression or restraint. Suppression is not the right translation. What do you mean by suppression? Why call it suppression? Do you mean you do not want your manas to think; you do not want your buddhi to function; you do not want your ego to function; you do not want your chitta to function? Do you want to suppress all the faculties of your mind? If you call it suppression or repression, then suppression and repression will lead your life. All suppressions bring misery. Suppression and repression are very dangerous for your mental life. Anything you suppress will come up in your dreams. How could Patanjali say you should suppress your mind and modifications? Actually, Patanjali says that you should cultivate your mind so your mind is in a state of perfect equilibrium. That is the true meaning. Nirodhah does not mean suppression; the actual meaning is control. There is a vast difference between suppression and control. When you are controlling something it means you are the master of that. If something is suppressed, it is bound to come up again, no matter how much ability you have to suppress, and it will control your life. To control does not mean to suppress or to stop. To control your mind does not mean you should not think. To stop thought is not the yogic way. To control does not mean not to do something or to stop functioning. It means knowing how to use a particular faculty, having conscious command of the various unknown powers within. *Control* means "to channel, to regulate, to strengthen, and to use properly." Mind should be controlled exactly as a rider controls the horse, not allowing the horse to run wild here and there. You should think the way you desire to think.

Nirodhah means to coordinate all the aspects of your mind, to cultivate your mind in a way so that your mind attains a state of equilibrium and tranquility, so that it is fit enough to attain the highest state of wisdom, samadhi. That is what yoga is. A mind that has cultivated a state of equilibrium is prepared for samadhi. You can attain samadhi only after you achieve nirodhah. Yoga means control. By gaining control over mind and its modifications you become a yogi. Learn to control your mind from within. When you control your mind from outside, you are a *bhogi*, not a yogi. Nirodhah does not mean to suppress your mind, feelings, or thoughts; you can never become a yogi that way. You will become sick. You should learn to have control over your mind, actions, speech, thoughts, emotions, and desires with the help of certain practices that Patanjali expounds.

You are not developing nirodhah because you lack *samkalpa-shakti*, determination. You cannot have the finest quality of mind because there is no coordination of the different faculties of the mind. If there is no coordination in my body and my hands tell me to go here, my mouth says to grab and eat this, and my eyes say to see that, what will happen to me? I will be operating like crazy. You lack nirodhah because you have not established coordination among chitta, manas, buddhi, and ahamkara. You have to understand and coordinate all aspects of the mind.

Those tendencies that are the characteristics of the lower mind should be checked first. You are tempted to have something but you do not have the means, so you want to steal it. Buddhi says that is not right for you, but ahamkara motivates you. *I want to have it. Nobody will know if I take it, so I'd better have it.* Unless buddhi is sharpened, unless you encourage the faculty within which decides, judges, and discriminates, you cannot guide manas. Again and again your buddhi says, *Do not do it, do not do it, do not do it!* Yet you do it, because manas is in the habit of motivating you. Manas controls your senses; the moment you wake up in the morning, you find you are not coordinated. You need to establish coordination between manas and buddhi. Try to understand what that coordination means.

I will tell you something that my master told me. I said to my master, "Suppose I want to have something or I am motivated to do something, how shall I practice control?"

He said, "It is very easy. The hanky is here and you would like to have it. Tell your mind to have it, but do not move your limbs. *Okay, mind. You can have it, but I will not allow my hands to move.* You have only known how much joy you will derive by picking up the hanky. Have you ever tried to understand how much joy you will derive if you do not pick it up? That you have not known. You do not know how much joy can be derived if you do not do something."

Your mind says, *Have it. It is something good. It looks beautiful. It is stimulating to the senses and soothing to the mind. Have it.* Your body is not your mind. If you cannot control your mind, at least you can control your physical body. *Okay, mind. You can have it. I cannot.*

If there is no cooperation between manas and its agents, the senses, you cannot have it. What will happen to that thought which was not realized? The thought will die, but it may come back again because it remains in the basement of your memories as an impression. It can motivate you again to do the same thing, and again you can say, *Okay, mind. You can have it.* This is discipline in action. You are disciplining the actions you perform through your limbs because you can see them. You can see your hands and you can hold your hands. You are disciplining your body and not your mind. *I am not going to have it.* Again and again mind says, *Take it. It is something beautiful and wonderful. It is gorgeous. You will enjoy it.* The body says *no.* In this way you are training your limbs. By training the indriyas, or senses, you can help manas. By training manas, you can help the indriyas, because the indriyas are subordinate to manas.

Rama Tirtha, a great sage, was very fond of apples. Anytime he saw good apples his mouth would water. It became an obsession for him and he used to think about apples all the time. Even if he were hungry, he would not eat unless he saw a good apple. His appetite came only because of the apples. He would first get an apple, and then he would eat.

He analyzed this and one day he said, "Okay, my dear apple. I am going to set you right." He kept an apple, cleaned it, washed it, cut it, put it in a plate, and decorated it nicely, but would not eat it. In a few days' time, that obsession was over.

When you start to discipline yourself, you will find a great joy, a great strength within yourself. Discipline does not mean that you should not do something. That is not my point. You should know four things when you discipline yourself: what to do, when to do it, how to do it, and where to do that. In these four, there is discrimination, buddhi's advice. If you ask, *What to do?* Buddhi advises. *When to do?* Buddhi advises you. Anything you do with the counsel of your buddhi will not be a problem. Buddhi is giving you skill, telling you where and how to do. When you do not consult your buddhi, or go against the counsel of your buddhi, you lose willpower.

No matter how civilized we may claim to be, human beings are still animals. If you remove the police force and the military in the world for three months, there will be hardly anyone left living in the world; there will be chaos all over. The police are guarding your morality. Discipline is being forced on you by the state because you are not disciplined. Patanjali teaches that when you learn to discipline yourself, and learn to live with yourself, then you will learn to live with others.

Those who are afraid of being disciplined or those who are afraid of following discipline cannot expect much from themselves. If you form the habit of wanting to do something, but you are not able to do it, you will have no willpower at all. First, you have to say, *I want to do it.* Then you say, *I can do it. I will do it. I have to do it, no matter what happens.* That is willpower. If you want to do something, do it. Stop thinking or doing anything else. Just do it, no matter what happens, no matter what the cost. That will create dynamic will and you will be able to do wonders. Your will is involved with your desires, your wishes, and wants. Many charms, attractions, and temptations come and try to control your life. If you become the victim of these charms and temptations, it means your willpower is weak. When your willpower is weak, you become a victim again and again and again. Then you become disgusted and condemn yourself. If you examine yourself within, all your desires are guided by motivations. If there is no willpower, you will find yourself a failure in life. When you want to do something, if you do it with a one-pointed mind, you will get results. If your mind is scattered and dissipated, then you will not get the results you desired. Learn to build your willpower.

What is that willpower? *Willpower* means "samkalpa-shakti." How to build that willpower? How is willpower necessary in your daily life, and how can you attain a state of wisdom so that you are successful within and without in your daily life? Patanjali says, *Yogash chitta-vritti-nirodhah.*

The more concentrated your mind is, the more you will have dynamic will. There are some things that you are very good at, and there are other things that you are not good at, because your willpower does not flow properly. Your mind does not concentrate properly because you have not trained your will. You should not set a goal impulsively and then disappoint yourself. First, determine your goal and resolve to attain it. Let the goal come to you. When Mohammad was ready, the mountain came to him; he did not go to the mountain. The mountain or your goal can also come to you. Make your mind one-pointed and let the object of your mind come back to you. The more one-pointed your mind becomes, the more powerful you become through willpower.

You do not understand willpower. You see your willpower only when something is taken away from you, when some adversity or obstacle comes in your life, because at that time your mind becomes very focused. When the mind is fully concentrated it creates willpower. The more dissipated your mind is, the more your willpower is weakened.

You should have dynamic willpower behind you to support you whenever you have problems. You can create willpower so that you can face all the calamities of life. You can develop willpower when you know how to organize the dissipated state of your mind. Your mind is being dissipated by your senses. When you can control your objective mind and you have trained the objective mind to remain constantly focused on some object, then you will have willpower. The more willpower you have, the more dynamic your personality will become.

When you develop willpower by concentrating your mind, you will have control over your mind and you will be fully aware of your capacity. You will be able to do things that are not within your usual limits. That which you did not previously understand, you will start to understand. Your memory will no longer be weak. You will stop doing things that you used to do habitually. You will know how to direct your mind whenever you want to. The world is very entangled in doing and not doing, not in *how* to do. The day you know how to do something, then those things you considered to be don'ts become something creative — how to do it.

Willpower is not a separate faculty. Willpower means perfect coordination among the different aspects and faculties of your mind. Patanjali is telling you to learn to control all the modifications of the mind so that all the aspects of your inner being start coordinating. If a person who wants to do something does it with full attention, that person has willpower. If a person who has willpower does not want to do something, nobody can motivate him to do it. If you do anything that you do not really want to do, it will bring tension. External tension can also give you many impressions that create diseases within. When you pay attention to your duties, you will not create tension and emotional problems. Tension is caused by lack of attention. If you do not want to do something, or if you have no interest in doing it, then do not do it. Otherwise, you weaken your willpower by doing it.

The external world can become disastrous if you do not know how to live. If you simply analyze and understand your situation, many of you will agree with me. You have created a situation for yourself in which you are living with someone with whom you do not want to live. You have bought a house and now you do not want to live in that house. You have educated yourself and you have mastered something that is not useful in the world. You have already done it. You have a job that you do not really like to do, but yet you are doing it. Every day you are putting yourself in situations that are not healthy for you because they create conflict and agony in your mind. You are doing things that you do not want to do. This creates tension in your daily life. Tension is not possible without conflict. Hard work itself never creates tension. Many people complain that they are suffering because of hard work. Nobody suffers from hard work no matter how much work they do. Wherever there is conflict there is pain. Conflict is the mother of all pains.

You think you are forced to do your duties. You often say, "My circumstances, my conditions, force me to do certain duties, so I am doing them. I am being controlled by my duties." You are a slave of your senses, your whims, and your habits. You have forgotten that your duties are self-created, yet you think that you are a victim of your duties. You always say, *This is my duty, so I have to do it.* You are very serious when you talk about your duties — your duty toward your partner, toward your children, toward your brothers and sisters. In this way duty brings tensions, stress, and chaos. If you constantly are doing something that you do not want to do, you are creating tension and preparing yourself for disease.

What is the solution? Should you not do your duties and run away to the Himalayas to run after a sadhu, like chasing a wild goose? What should you do? You cannot live in the world peacefully and happily without doing your duties, so you should learn to do your duties with love. Do not do work to which you are not paying attention. Create interest in what you are doing. If you learn to do that, then you will not be led by your unconscious habits. When you are doing something unconsciously, it means that unconscious habit has control over you. Pay attention from morning till evening, whatever you do. By paying attention in the external world, you are slowly training your mind. The more you pay attention, the more you become aware. If you are paying attention to something that you should not want to do, you will hate to do it and you will not do it. If you are paying attention to something that you want to do, you will take an interest in doing it, you will enjoy doing it, and it will not give you tension. You do many things in the world in the name of enjoyment, but actually you do not enjoy them. You will enjoy them more if you know the attitude that you should have toward the objects of the world: be conscious. If you are not conscious of the wealth that you have, the potentials that you have, and the things that you enjoy, they are of no use to you. You should be fully conscious of the things that you enjoy. To experience even the smallest enjoyment of this world you need to have a one-pointed mind. When the mind is distracted and you do something but you are thinking of something different, that is not enjoyment. It is the nature of mind to attend to one thing at a time. Whatever you do, your mind should be there: that is enjoyment.

Remind yourself every morning to watch your actions. Sometimes you do not want to do something, yet you do it because of deep-rooted habits, even though you understand that it is not right. Many times you force yourself to do things that you do not want to do. If you go on doing this, then your mind stops moving with your body. If the mind moves, the body also moves, but if the body moves, it is not necessarily true that the mind moves. There is a word in Sanskrit — *apta*. Apta means that your speech and your actions follow the way you think. In ancient times everybody was called apta. Now apta has degenerated to *aap*. In India we use the word *aap* for everyone out of reverence, but no one is truly apta because of lack of discipline.

Many wives and husbands pretend in their love relationships. You may not want to laugh and talk, but if your husband wants you to laugh, you will laugh. Sometimes you want to be calm and quiet. It is not necessary for you to be a laughing doll all the time.

If somebody expects you to laugh and you do not feel like it, do not laugh. If you pretend all the time, you create a double personality. When your behavior is different than the way you think, it creates illness. Eighty to ninety percent of diseases are because of this problem. You are doing something, but actually you are not doing it with a one-pointed mind because you lack proper training. Though you are here, your mind is somewhere else. You can experiment with this: wherever you go you will find that your mind is not there. You are forcing your body to move, going against your will. You have not understood the relationship of body and mind. You should always remember that the whole of the mind is not in the body, but the whole of the body is in the mind. Mind does not remain within the limitations of your bodily needs only. That is why a human being is not completely satisfied by bodily needs. Mind is not limited to the body only, but the body is within the limitations of the mind.

Human beings have tremendous capacity. You have all the powers. You are fully equipped with potentials. If you learn to understand those potentials and know how to apply them, you can be successful. First, you should be fully aware that you have potentials. You encounter only that superficial part of mind that is known to you, that which has been polished by you. You do not trust yourself. You tell others how nice you are. You do not want anyone to know how bad you are. You do not want to feel that you are bad, yet you understand from within, and when you touch only that part, you suddenly become disappointed and disperse the idea that you have potentials. You should be aware that you have the capacity to have control and command over the modifications of your mind. If you are not in touch with your potentials, you cannot have that faith which is based on reason and facts, that faith and conviction that have gone through the process of intellectualization by your buddhi. That conviction tells you, *Here I am. This is like this.* Then you do not doubt it.

How can you come in touch with the potentials that you have? Look at how powerful the mind is, how it controls your life. You have to realize that the power of self-condemnation that makes you so sad and disappoints you, is also a power of the mind. How do you condemn yourself? You say, *How bad I am. How dirty I am. How useless I am. How hopeless I am. I am very small. I know very little. I am not physically strong. I do not have enough money.* You make yourself go toward smallness.

That which distracts you is the negative power of mind. Everyday you need somebody to make you aware of how wonderful you are, how beautiful you are, how good you are, because you are not aware of that. You will have to recognize the negative power of the mind and how it torments you and troubles you. You argue with your thoughts. One side protects you, the other side attacks. You have completely shattered your nervous system because you do this the whole day. A part of your mind becomes very defensive, while the other part attacks you negatively. You call it intellectualism. It divides you into two parts. *Oh, he is such a bad man. No, he is not a bad man. Why not? He is a bad man.* After ten minutes you say, *What the hell am I doing to myself? If he is a bad man, let him be. If he is a good man, let him be. Why am I becoming bad by thinking about him?* You identify yourself with your negative thoughts and create hell for yourself.

The part of the mind that torments you is very powerful. Patanjali says this is not you. You are not only mind. Your entire personality, your whole life is not the mere mind, so do not go with the advice of that mind which has been negatively strengthened and is negatively functioning. Mind is your instrument and you have the power in you to control all the modifications of your mind. Once you have done it, then the center of consciousness will reveal itself to you. You are worrying for enlightenment and liberation without understanding the power of mind. You must realize the power of mind and how negative it can be. The same power you find in children who are very destructive. You scold them and you spank them because you are annoyed and you cannot cope with their energy. You do not know how to deal with them so you spank them and then you feel disgusted and disappointed. The same power could be diverted toward creativity and that could become a great power. The mind has dual powers—one is destructive and the other is creative. The destructive power is: *How bad I am, how dirty I am, how small I am, how horrible I am, how lonely I am. Nobody likes me. I am all alone.* You always want somebody to help you, to appreciate and admire you. You do not realize yourself. You are blind to reality. You do not want to see the reality because you are afraid and because you have been condemning yourself.

Negative thoughts, uncontrolled thoughts, and passive thoughts can all be harmful to you. Thinking plays a great part as far as physical diseases are concerned. There are many diseases for which there is no cure because you are creating them from within. Most of the psychosomatic diseases are like that. You create problems for yourself. Most diseases are self-created. The source of all diseases is called conflict within and without. In psychosomatic diseases, changes in physiological and biological reactions occur because of your thoughts and your emotions. If you have many conflicts within, those conflicts constantly blast your nervous system, and you suffer. If you want to understand your mind, you have to understand your thoughts. Your thoughts are based on your emotions. Your thought forms are responsible for creating diseases because you are controlled by your thought patterns. A thought pattern comes, affects your mind, and goes away. You are affected by that particular thought. If it is negative, it depresses you; if it is positive, it inspires you. If you brood on that thought pattern, you start identifying with it, forgetting the reality and forgetting yourself. You can obtain freedom from that negativity. You should try to control the thinking process by not allowing your thoughts to go toward negativity. You can slowly try to understand the good points in yourself and awaken the positivity in your life. Then, you will realize how foolish you were to be controlled by those thought forms that you have created for yourself.

Once you understand the inner functioning of your mind, you will come to know that you constantly create problems for yourself and that you also constantly heal yourself. If you understand the functioning of the mind, you will know that psychosomatic diseases can easily be healed. There are many healing agents within. Willpower is one of the means for healing. If you have a healthy mind, that healthy mind itself will protect you from many illnesses. There are certain illnesses such as infections and viral diseases for which you need medical treatment. Even then a healthy mind will help you.

Some people get well quickly because their mind is healthy; others take a long time.

Modern psychology is aware of the negative power of the mind but does not know how to awaken the positive power. The day modern people come to know the method of awakening the positive power of the mind, they will find that mind can be used for healing purposes also. I have demonstrated that I could create a tumor in my body just by thinking negatively. That shows how a negative mind can immediately create problems in the body. When I started thinking positively, it disappeared.[2] It is possible for anyone to understand both sides of the mind. If you can train yourself, you can remain free from diseases.

Do not condemn yourself. Do not think that you cannot progress or that you cannot help yourself. Power is one and the same. How can negative power be modified and transformed into positive power? The power that you use in condemning yourself, in negative thinking, can transform your personality if you use it in positive thinking. You can become anything you want to become. Do not think that you are too small and you do not have power. You have the power to become divine.

[2] See Appendix A, Tumors.

In Indian history there was one sage called Valmiki. He was like St. Paul. He was one of the worst criminals and he became one of the greatest sages. He used to rob people, especially swamis. He had a desire to rob swamis because he thought that swamis were a burden to the nation and to themselves. Whenever he saw a group of swamis he would loot them and then kill them. Why did he do that? He was a strong man. He found that by looting he could easily fulfill his personal responsibility of taking care of his wife and children. One day when he was looting a group of swamis he met a sage. One swami said to him, "Wait. You can do whatever you want to do, but first find out who will be responsible for your karma, for your actions. You are doing this for your family members. You have to do your duties, but go to your wife and children and ask them if they will be responsible for your karma. Just go and ask them."

He said, "My wife loves me. She will be responsible for them. My children also love me immensely."

The swami said, "Go ahead and ask. I promise we will not move. We will wait for you."

He went home and he told his wife, "I rob people and kill them. Will you share the consequences of this?"

She said, "You are a fool. Why should I share the consequences?"

Valmiki then went to his children and asked, "I am committing crimes. Will you reap the fruits of my actions?"

They said, "No. You are our father. You have to do it. You are doing your duty. You are doing your actions. You are responsible for reaping the fruits of your actions, not us."

He came back and told the sage what they had said. The sage said, "Now, understand that you are responsible for the fruits of your actions, not other people. You are committing crimes just to feed your children, to look after your children, and to please your wife. This is not going to help you." Suddenly he became aware of the Reality. After that the same Valmiki became a sage.

You should accept the responsibility you have toward people, but you should discriminate and understand the actions you are doing. Will they be helpful for you or not? There are many such examples of transformation of personality. Total transformation is possible, just as on the way to Damascus, Saul's personality was transformed. When you understand and become aware of the Reality within, your personality will be transformed.

You have to understand your mind properly in its totality. You have to know yourself both within and without. It is very easy to know yourself provided you want to. You are trying to escape. You are afraid of knowing yourself. From childhood onward you are trained to see and examine things in the external world. Nobody teaches you to look within, to find within, or to see within. You are a stranger to yourself, and others are also strangers to you. Two strangers make promises to each other, smile, talk, and establish a home, and then create disaster for themselves in society. This is going on all over the world. Life as it is seems to be summed up with one word—relationship—relationship in the external world and relationship within. How is your body related to your breathing being, to your thinking being, and then to your consciousness? How is individual consciousness related to other individuals and to the whole universe?

Although the body and mind are two separate units, they work together. Your body is related to your mind with the help of two guards called inhalation and exhalation. The day they do not work together, these two units fall apart. The mortal part (your body, your breath, and your conscious mind) separates from the partially mortal self (the unconscious mind) and the immortal self (the *jiva* or individual soul). When the mortal self is separated from the partially mortal self and the immortal self, that is death. Death means separation of the body, senses, and conscious mind from the unconscious mind and the soul. Death occurs the moment the breath stops functioning. People worry and talk about death so much and are so afraid of it, they do not want to think about or understand or analyze what death is. Death is a habit of the body. Death is very peaceful, but fear of death is very painful.

Let me tell you one thing: if you are waiting to die, you will be sorry. Death never changes your inner personality; it never helps you. Just as sleep does not change your financial condition, death does not change your personality. You have to learn to transform your personality right here and now by understanding not only body, breath, and conscious mind, but also both parts of the unconscious — active and latent. Death means separation, not complete annihilation. You still live after you cast off your body. Which part of you lives? The unconscious mind, the reservoir of all your samskaras — the impressions of your merits and demerits, whatever you have done — continues to live. The unconscious mind is a vehicle for the soul. All of your acts dwell in this reservoir as a memory. It is just like starting another day. Today you are the same as you were yesterday. Sleep makes you forget some things, but that which is useful you still remember. Those impressions that you stored from your past — from yesterday, from the day before yesterday, from last year, from your whole life, from several lives — every impression that you received in the past, you have stored in the unconscious mind.

Those who are yogis recognize the people they have known before. For them the previous life is just like yesterday. It is an interesting subject: my master used to check me when he was training me. It became a very serious problem for me when he taught me this. I would meet somebody whom I had known in a previous life. That person who in a prior life was my great enemy, in this life had become a great friend. Why? To fulfill his animosity. The person who was a great enemy, now became a friend, and the person who was a friend, now became an enemy. It was very difficult for me to adjust: I was suspicious of everybody and I could not relate. Many times the impressions of two or three lifetimes came in front of me and they were very vivid.

You do not go to heaven or hell after death, but you live in your habit patterns. You go with your habit patterns, with your unconscious. That is a vehicle for the individual soul, or jiva. The unconscious mind stays with you. You are called an individual because you have an individual vehicle that has been formed by your individual habit patterns, impressions, desires, and motivations. One human being's habits are not like the habits of any other human being. You are different, not because of different thinking, but because of different behavior, different desires, motivations, impressions, and *samskaras*. All individuals have the vehicle of the unconscious even after death. That is where impressions, samskaras, and desires remain. Without knowing your *samskaras* you cannot purify yourself, you cannot train yourself, you cannot utilize the wisdom that you have carried from your past lives or from your childhood.

Who created these samskaras for you? You resign and say that God has created you as you are and nothing can be done. You think you cannot be transformed, you cannot be helped, so you pray. Suppose food is offered to you and you are hungry and you eat. You could say, *Oh, Lord, this is your grace.* That would be very good. Instead you say, *Lord, digest my food. Please chew for me, please circulate my blood properly.* This is not going to help you. It is just like trying to churn oil from sand. A human being has the power to understand his own existence and the universal existence, that eternal Truth which exists itself.

Your Personality, Your Character, is Composed of Your HABITS

Patanjali teaches us to learn to understand ourselves in a very simple way. If you want to study your samskaras and what you have done in the past, there is no need to count them. If you want to know what your personality is and how to help yourself, and you decide to count your bad qualities, you are only strengthening those qualities. You will not help yourself; that is not the way to understand your personality. Your personality, your character, is composed of your habits. Nobody told you to become as you are; you have done it yourself. Your face is the way you wanted to paint it. Whatever you are is your own making, just as you have chosen the color of the clothes you are wearing. You are the architect of your own character, your own being. You can know yourself by trying to observe your deep habits.

Many times a thought comes in the mind of a sadhaka when he practices that now he is purified. He thinks he does not need any more austerities or purification practices. Suddenly he finds himself going back again to the same past grooves, the same habit patterns. When you examine your personality you realize that your personality is nothing but deep-rooted habits. You try your best to change your personality but you cannot, because of these habit patterns. A habit is a powerful thing. That which you have done repeatedly is your habit. Habit is the basis of your character and your personality. You want to change your whole personality without understanding your habit patterns. Habit patterns are very strong. When you do something again and again, that action of yours is being stored in chitta, the storehouse of merits and demerits. That becomes motivation for you to do something else. If you do something again and again, it will become a strong habit. Habit patterns—habits of overeating, of being obstinate, of not agreeing with your husband or wife— are very strong parts of the unconscious mind. At lunchtime, without even looking at the clock, everybody gets up and goes for lunch, just out of habit. There are people who wake up at the same time every morning, no matter what time they have gone to bed. They have formed a habit, so they cannot sleep after that. Unconsciously you get up at night and begin to bite your nails. Some people impulsively go to the refrigerator at night and eat. Other people keep candies beside their pillows. This is the same impulse. All these habits have been formed because of a lack of control over mind and its modifications.

I will tell you how powerful habit patterns are. My master used to love one of the rulers of India and he was one of the worst men I had ever met. He used to drink a lot. But whenever he felt any sadness he would come and sit near my master. Many times I asked my master, "Why do you allow this animal to come and waste your time?"

"Yes," he said. "You do not know. A part of this man is very good."

"Can you help him?" I asked.

He said, "I would like to, but he doesn't listen to anyone."

One morning my master suddenly said, "Look. Such and such Maharaja ruler is going to die in an accident tomorrow. Let us protect him. At least let us do our own part."

I said, "If you want to protect him, then we should go. If you cannot, we should not go."

He said, "Let's go."

So he called the ruler and his wife both and said, "Sit down. I have never asked you for anything. Will you give me something if I ask you?"

They both said, "Yes. You can have our palace and our wealth."

He said, "No, I don't need that garbage. What shall I do with it? It is my order as your teacher, as your guru, or even as a stranger to tell you not to go out of your home tomorrow. Call your guards and everybody. You should be locked in your room and not allowed to go out. You are going to die tomorrow at five o'clock, and I want to protect you. I am fighting with death. Will you cooperate with me?"

They promised. I was sitting next to them. I quietly said to my master, "What is going to happen?"

He said, "I am doing my duty, but they will not listen to me."

I said, "What is the use of doing this?"

He said, "This will be a lesson for other students."

He was kept under lock and key and guards were deputed. My master said, "Look, guards. No matter what happens, no matter how much he screams, don't let him out."

That man used to keep one Colt pistol with him always. Even though he had guards, he still kept the pistol. And he was an alcoholic. So, at five o'clock he was supposed to die. At three o'clock he became insane and started drinking. He drank two bottles of whiskey and then he said, "I am your ruler. If you keep me captive, I will see that you are all put behind the bars." And he told his wife, "You are my wife. Tomorrow I am getting married to another woman."

Everybody was afraid. They opened the lock. He pulled his wife by the hand into the car and started the car. "You are my wife. Be with me."

She knew that something was going to happen. It was at four-thirty that he started his car downhill and smashed the car. The car was completely smashed and they both were killed. My master and I were sitting somewhere. He said, "What shall I do? They would not listen to me."

Many times you know that you are not doing that which should be done, or that you should not do something, yet you do it, because manas has led you to form habit patterns. For instance, what is alcoholism? First you drink consciously. When you continue to drink regularly for some time then it becomes your habit. A habit is that which goes down deep to the unconscious, over which you have no control. Habits filter down to the unconscious from the conscious mind. Even though you do not want to drink and you know you should not drink because the doctor said it is bad for your health, your unconscious habits still motivate you to do it. Sugar is like poison for a diabetic patient, but I have seen diabetic patients being irresponsible and eating too much sugar. They even steal sugar sometimes, although they know it is injurious. Their habit causes them to do it. The doctor says, "Do not drink, do not eat sugar, do not overeat, get some exercise." You understand these are good suggestions, so why don't you follow them? It's because of bad habits. Even though buddhi is telling you what to do, you are not listening. This means there is no perfect coordination between the two faculties—buddhi and manas. The intellect tells you not to do it, yet you do it because you are habitual. You need to learn to sharpen your buddhi and take suggestions from buddhi, which always guides you on the right path. When you do something repeatedly, it means that your intellect did not function properly because it was never trained. You have only trained the part of intellect that helps to guide you in your daily life, but that intellect is not going to help you when you have formed a deep habit. The habits that you have formed are internal. Again and again your mind is looking for external guidance, but you are not training your internal states. Many times you say, *I don't want to know that.* You do not want to know things, even though you already know them, because that part of you makes you sad, and you do not want to face it. You are afraid to know your own self. Try to face all the corners of your inner life by understanding your habits. Once a habit is strong, even if the intellect wants to help you, it cannot.

It is not difficult to be healthy. It's a very easy and simple thing. But first you have to decide. Do you really want to be healthy? Put the question before yourself. You can be healthy. The block is your habits. You can easily understand your habits if you want to. In one day's time you can become aware of all your habits — those strong habits that motivate you to act in the world and make you feel sad or joyful. If you can work with your habit patterns, you can do anything. You can enjoy physical, mental, and spiritual health.

The nature of mind is to flow in the grooves of past experiences, and you cannot get out of those grooves. That is why the past becomes so dominant in your life. You do not want to go to your past habits; you want to transform your personality. Repeated actions create grooves in the mind, and then the mind, in its spontaneity and profundity, habitually flows to those grooves that have been created. The more you do something, the more deeply you create a groove in your unconscious mind and a time will come when you will become helpless to change it. Finally, you will give up. You think you cannot do anything about it because it is your habit.

Yoga science teaches that we can create new grooves. It has nothing to do with the senses. If you understand how you formed the habit, it will become easy for you to change. If you create new grooves and allow your mind to flow to the new grooves, then you can change your habits and transform your personality. You will have to repeat those new impressions again and again and again so that mind starts flowing from the old grooves to the new grooves. If you give me a bucket full of water and I sprinkle it everywhere, nothing will happen. If I pour all the water at one place, it will make a groove there. To break a bad habit you need to form a good habit. You can easily do away with a bad habit and establish a good habit. Habits are very strong, but you can slowly change them. It may take time, but you can work with yourself. If you know how to deal with your unconscious mind, then you will know how to direct your conscious mind. You can change your entire personality by changing your habits and replacing them with different habits.

FOUR FOUNTAINS: Become Aware of Your HABITS

You can become aware of your habits by studying how you manage the four primitive fountains. This is a very practical way of understanding yourself. If you study all the living kingdoms, you will learn that any creature that has come to the level of manifestation, anything that is subject to growth, has the four primitive urges — to take food, to sleep, to do sex, and to preserve oneself. These are instinctive desires. As far as these primitive forces are concerned, animals, human beings, and even plants are one and the same. Plants sleep; human beings sleep. Plants do sex; human beings do sex. Plants have a nervous system, though it is not as sensitive as the human nervous system. If you cut a plant, the plant "weeps." Animals also take food, sleep, do sex, and have a sense of self-preservation. The difference between animals and human beings is that animals are completely controlled by instincts. They do not do sex at just any time like human beings do. The sexual behavior of animals is controlled by nature: there is a fixed time, a mating season. This is not the case with human beings, who will mate anytime, anywhere. There is a vast difference: your appetites, your emotions, your thoughts, your activities, are only partially controlled by nature. You have the power of discrimination, the power of understanding, the power of control. You are responsible for your own actions.

The primitive fountains have their impact on the human mind and body. You have to learn how to deal with the problems that are brought forward by these basic urges. First, examine your inclinations toward food, sleep, sex, and self-preservation. Patanjali teaches that you must regulate all your appetites.

If you decide to observe the way your mind manages the desire for food, you can ask yourself many questions: When you are hungry can you wait for a while? If you do not take food in time, what happens? Why do you eat food? Are you concerned about how food will affect your mind, not only your body? Are you considering if that food will damage or hurt you? If you are given junk food, are you tempted to eat it? Can you throw away that junk food if you know that nutritious food is good for your health, even though the nutritious food is not so tempting as the junk food? Your desire for food and your acquired tastes are two different things. How are your tastes related to your desire for food? Are you at the mercy of your sense of taste? When you become a victim of your appetites, then the value of your food decreases. Train your mind to go toward nutrition when eating food.

After experimenting for millions of years, humanity has not yet found the best way to achieve good nutrition. You all eat food, yet you do not really understand the method of living and being. A holy man once said that if you know how to control the mind's holes, you are a very advanced person. For a few minutes I did not understand what he meant. Most physical diseases come into your body from one hole — the mouth. The mouth is the dirtiest part of the body. If you do not regularly clean your teeth, the function of your liver will be affected. If you do not keep your mouth clean, it will be a source of constant disease.

What should be your attitude when you eat food? The right attitude for taking food is: I eat to live but I do not live to eat. Develop the attitude that good food is needed for healthy living. If you eat the same food as someone else but have different attitudes, the effect of the food will be different. Eating good food alone is not sufficient; the other issue is *how* to take food.

Whatever you eat, eat on time, and enjoy the meal. Taking food on time is a very good habit. Doctors are very intelligent and skilled people but they have no time. They develop physical illnesses because they cannot regulate their sleeping and eating habits. No matter what happens, form the habit of taking food at a time when your profession does not intervene. It is not necessary to take food at one o'clock every day. If you are working at one o'clock, set another time. I do not recommend eating too much food at one time for the whole day. It is better to eat two or three times a day rather than taking only one meal. I also do not recommend wasting the whole day in eating six or seven meals. If you do this, you are never resting your poor intestines.

Form the habit of not drinking water or liquids while taking food. You can take juice or water half an hour earlier or after eating. If you have to take liquid, then there is another way: you can take liquid as a food. My feeling is you can take milk as a food, not as a drink. To drink something and to take food are two different processes.

In all the great traditions there is a custom of saying grace before a meal. This has some significance; gastric juices and saliva are both important for digestion, and saying grace gives you time to calm down and create saliva and gastric juices before you start eating. If the gastric juices are deficient, you cannot digest food properly and you will have problems. You do not know how to consciously produce sufficient gastric juice and saliva so that your food is digested properly. Even if you take the best vitamins and the most complete diet possible, if you do not create sufficient gastric juice and saliva, you cannot digest it. It is important to think about calories and the nutritional value of food, but you cannot digest even the best food if you have digestive problems. The digestive enzymes and secretions are dependent on the proper functioning of the endocrine system, which is controlled by your emotions. Simple, fresh food that is full of nutrients is very good for health, but first your thinking and attitudes should be improved. Your thinking is related to your emotions and can create problems for you. There was one case in Germany in 1956. A woman whose husband wanted to divorce her became very emotionally upset while breastfeeding her child. When she became so nervous, the child turned blue and collapsed. The child had been quite healthy previously. When you become emotional your biochemistry changes and creates toxins. Regularity and cheerfulness are very important when taking food.

Make the atmosphere at your home cheerful. Do not fight while taking food. You can fight with your wife or husband later on, but not while eating. That is a very unhealthy thing. Don't spank your child before or while eating. It is very bad for the child's digestion if the child is weeping and you are pushing food into her mouth. When you are feeling depressed, or you are fighting with your husband or wife, or arguing with your children, please do not eat. If you are full of anxiety, do not eat. If you eat in those conditions, you are bound to create toxins instead of giving energy to your body. When you are in an abnormal emotional state that is beyond your control, you should not eat. Wait until you become calm or the food will be converted into toxins. Life is very short. While there is time you should enjoy every moment. If you are not cheerful, no matter how delicious the food is, you will not be able to digest it.

I was taught to take food alone my whole life. I am not tossed by external conditions nor do I crave for anyone's company in life. I enjoy my food in cheerfulness. Cheerfulness is essential for those who live in the world and lead a householder's life. If you are not in a good mood, don't eat. Learn to be cheerful so that your biochemistry is prepared to digest your food.

However much you eat, you should be cheerful while eating and learn to chew your food properly. Many people swallow food without really chewing it. If you chew each bite thirty-five times, you will be able to digest whatever you eat. If you have the habit of eating too much, eat as much as you want but chew it repeatedly. This will help you to avoid overeating. You overeat because you don't take time to relish your food. You just fill up your belly and it keeps expanding. You don't pay attention to your meal. You live to eat, yet you don't have time to eat. You eat too much because your diet is not sufficient and does not have enough nutrients, minerals, and vitamins. There is something missing somewhere; if your diet is balanced, you will not overeat. You overeat when either your diet is imbalanced or your mind is imbalanced. Those who overeat are trying to substitute for something. There is a law of compensation in the human body and mind. Observe your capacity: overeating is a sign of insecurity and it comes from the mental level. Eating too much is a disease, and is very injurious. You should eat according to your physical needs. Do not exceed your capacity.

Whatever your food, you should have the attitude that you like the food you are eating. If you go to some party, you feel that you have to eat or your friend will be annoyed. Don't force yourself to take food to please others. You are not helping others by taking food. When you do not want to eat, don't eat. Don't force yourself or others to eat too much. If you force yourself every day to eat a little bit more food, eventually you will find that your thyroid gland is affected. Then you will find your weight starts increasing. Being overweight is the foremost disease in all the diseases I have studied, so don't eat too much. Learn to eat whatever you think is better for you. Slowly work with yourself. People who eat the whole day do not really have a physical problem, although physicians say it is because of the thyroid gland. In reality it is an emotional problem. Some people get up at two in the morning and eat, or they put food underneath their pillow so they are assured of having something to eat throughout the night because of emotional problems.

In the West there is a custom of drinking a little wine before the meal as an appetizer. It helps in digesting the food. In yoga science you don't need any appetizer. Lying down on the left side for ten to fifteen minutes after eating is good for your digestion. But when you take too much food, and then sleep and snore and dream, how can you interpret those dreams? Those dreams will not reveal your personality; rather they will reveal the bad effects of food. Sometimes nightmares occur after eating too much food too late. Either you have eaten too much, or you have done sex immediately after eating, and then you have slept. Many people have the habit of eating late at night. It is harmful to eat late and then go to bed. There should be at least a three to four-hour gap between eating and going to sleep. The evening meal should be very light and you should eat your meal four hours before you go to sleep. Going to sleep right after eating can cause many diseases.

It is a tradition to eat three to four meals daily and to sleep for eight to ten hours. Nobody really understands why we need eight to ten hours of "punishment," but that has become a part of human habit and tradition. Eight to ten hours of sleep is a waste of your life. You have a great opportunity during the waking state, but when you go to sleep you lose touch with the waking state and misuse the time that you have by oversleeping. You could meditate, you could study, you could write, or, if you are capable, you could help others.

Early in my training I was trained to not sleep uselessly. Sleep means inertia. How can you sleep peacefully if you have to attain something in life? I never consider myself an adept or a great swami, but I cannot sleep for a long time. The moment I nap someone says from within, *Have you come to this world to sleep? What do you do after death? You sleep for a*

*long time. You remain in an unconscious state. You have
come to the conscious state to attain something, to regain
something. You are wasting your time and your energy.
Wake up!* I look at the clock and see it is not yet three
o'clock, which is my time. It is only 2:30. And I think,
Half an hour more for my practice? Come on. Sit down!
Because I have that fire within I do not want to sleep
and I cannot sleep even if I want to. When I sleep, I
sleep for seventeen days without break. But that is
not sleep. I cannot spend more than two and a half
hours sleeping or I feel guilty, as though I have
committed a crime. My duties are so heavy that I will
not be able to complete my work if I sleep. If I cannot
complete my work, my conscience will tell me, *Why
are you eating? What is this you are doing? Seeing this
person and that person, everybody touching your feet,
and you are not doing your work?* I go on working day
and night for many days. No one can cope with me
because I know how to rest. I can even rest in the
bathroom, just sitting. I'm not joking. I take ten to
fifteen-minutes' rest, then come back fresh, and again
work.

I do not know how you people can sleep so
much. Why do you want to waste your time and
energy? Have you come to this life to sleep? You were
better off when you were in deep sleep, before you
were born. Curtail your sleep. Sleep can be brought
under your control. When you know that you have
only a little time, you will be able to sleep deeply during
that time. Your mind says, *I do not have much time; I
have to sleep now because I have some important things
to do afterwards.* Then, the moment you lie down you
will sleep. When you have too much time to sleep and
you go to bed, you do not get sleep. You hurt yourself
because you do not know a few things that can help

in organizing your internal states. By knowing them you can maintain good health and a sound mind. Sleep can be brought under control by knowing the art of sleep.

If you drink too much water before going to bed, you will have nightmares. Go to the bathroom to urinate before you go to bed. You should also have *panch-snan*—a short bath of the face, hands, and feet.

If you know how to regulate the motion of your lungs, you can enjoy sleep more, for irregular breathing disturbs you when you are asleep. Those who are not acquainted with the subject should ask someone to watch the way they breathe when they are asleep. When your partner is quietly sleeping, watch patiently. Sometimes he or she will inhale quickly and then have a long exhalation, or alternately, a long inhalation and short exhalation. Then, the whole motion of the lungs is irregular, which affects the vagus nerve and the autonomic nervous system.

Some people suffer on account of insomnia because their conscious mind remains very active and preoccupied. They want to sleep but they cannot. Most of the time it takes you ten to fifteen minutes to fall asleep. Why should you take so much time to sleep? It means you have not decided. If you want to sleep, just sleep. If you are determined to sleep, you should be able to sleep soon. You should not have to make extra effort to sleep. If you tell yourself that punctually at ten o'clock you will sleep, why don't you sleep? Whenever you are trying to sleep, tell yourself that now you have to sleep. You go to sleep when you are tired. You should not sleep because you are tired. Children who are tired cannot sleep for some time and they will cry. When they have cried for some time, then they will go to sleep. They are not sleeping because their body is tired. They are sleeping because they have wept so much. If you sleep because your body is tired, you will feel restless and you will have nightmares. You should understand this point: It is not necessary for you to be tired to sleep. You should rest for the next day, not because you are tired. It is also not necessary for you to sleep conventionally. You don't have to sleep because it is ten o'clock. "Come on, children. Go to bed. You have to wake up early in the morning," you say. That is a good thing, but you do not train yourself that way. When you go to bed, prepare yourself for the next day.

Try to get up early in the morning before sunrise. Getting up early in the morning between three to five a.m. is a very good habit. Try to form that habit. That is the best time to break inertia. Don't waste your time at bars and parties late at night. All those parties reflect on your face in the morning, and then you have to paint your face to look beautiful. If you want to break the inertia of sloth and laziness, learn to wake up on time in the morning. No matter what time I go to bed, I have to wake up on time. That is one thing I have maintained in my life. I told myself that if sloth controls my life, it is of no use living. Don't allow sloth to control your life. Sloth is the greatest enemy you could have. And nobody can help you there. It is injurious to oversleep. It is not possible to actually sleep more than three and a half hours. Delta waves, which indicate deep sleep, cannot last more than three to three and a half hours. Much of the rest of the time you are tossing and turning in bed. Sometimes you wake up, and then you go back to disturbed sleep; sometimes you are dreaming. You are disturbing your metabolism and you call it rest. That which is truly deep sleep does not last more than three and a half hours. You cannot actually sleep for ten hours unless you are under anesthesia.

You should sleep for an appointed period of time. *I will sleep for one hour because I have to work later on.* This is voluntary sleep. Before you go to bed decide, *Today I will sleep. At two-thirty I have to do this. At three o'clock I have to sit in meditation. In the morning I have to work. I have to share my time with other people because I am a human being, a member of society. I have to do this. I cannot deny others. I have to take deep rest. I will not be able to pay attention to my work if I am not rested.* The last resolution you should have at night before going to bed should be: *I will wake up fresh at three o'clock or four o'clock, according to my schedule. I will go to deep sleep and no one will be able to disturb my sleep.*

Samkalpa, determination of your mind, is very important. I just ask myself before I go to bed to have deep sleep and to get up at five o'clock. There should not be a single minute's delay. There was a time when I had some delay — ten, five, four minutes' delay — but now it does not happen. If I determine that I have to get up at five o'clock, I will get up at exactly five o'clock. This is the predetermined way of enjoying sleep. Instead, you set an alarm and go to sleep, or you ask the operator to give you a buzz. This way you ignore the potentials that you have within. A few minutes before you go to sleep give instructions to your mind. Ask yourself to give complete rest to your mind and to get up early in the morning at such and such time. Determine first that you will sleep and that you will sleep for a certain number of hours. No alarm, no telephone aid, no servant, or no neighbor should be engaged to wake you up. It is possible for you to do that. The first few days you might not have complete success, but later on you will. This internal alarm system will triple your potentials.

If you learn to use the time when you are fully awake, and learn how to quiet your mind and expand your consciousness, you can reduce the amount of dream time and sleep you need. I lived with Gandhiji and many other yoga masters and teachers and I observed them. They did not sleep more than two and one-half hours and yet they were very healthy. Too much sleep is not necessary, and does not offer you much. After sleeping for many hours your personality does not change, nor does your economic condition. Sleep gives you only partial rest. It does not give deep rest to the totality of your being. Sleep gives rest to the brain, the nervous system, the muscles, and the conscious mind. It does not give rest to your unconscious mind or to the totality of your mind. When you wake up you know that you have not fully rested. If the mind does not get rest through any other means, then mental diseases start to affect the nervous system and then the body. Do not expect too much from sleep or from anesthesia. Anesthesia relieves your pain when a surgeon is operating upon you, but it cannot relieve the pain of your mind. Mental pain is more serious than physical pain. You need to be free from all pains and miseries.

You should also create a certain attitude when you go to sleep. After all the enjoyments of the world, you want to enjoy your sleep. If you do not sleep, all your other enjoyments will not have any real value. Sleep is the highest enjoyment that you have.

Mahatma Gandhi said, "Before I go to bed, I go through two things: prayer and repentance."

I said, "Repentance is a very bad thing."

He said, "Wait. Let me explain what it really is. Prayer and repentance purify the way of the soul and lead you to your goal finally. To whom are you praying? Not to any God, not to the sun, moon, or stars. You are praying to yourself, to the finest part of yourself. You are purifying your lower mind and making your lower mind aware of your higher nature. You are praying to your higher nature."

"And repentance?"

"Before mind prays, mind says, *Well, I have done this and I have done that. I am not able to pray.* Repentance comes first; prayer comes afterward."

Gandhi meant a certain kind of repentance. If you keep repeating, *I did this, I did that*, you will become weak. This is not what he meant. *Repentance* simply means "not to repeat." If you have done something of which your conscience did not approve, determine that you will not do it again. This is similar to confession in the Catholic religion. You are letting out your hidden weaknesses, bringing them to the surface where you can deal with them. The therapist does the same thing. You can do it yourself in the process of self-therapy. Before going to bed, ask the accountant within you to furnish the accounts. The accountant is not afraid of you and will clearly tell you. If you are a coward, you will not do it because you know you have not been doing things the way you want, according to your convictions. You will have to face all that sooner or later. *Okay, tomorrow when my day starts, I will not repeat this, no matter what happens. For at least one day I will see.* For this you have to decide. *I will do it. I can do it. I have to do it. I am going to do it.* This will build your determination. Children who are afraid of the darkness, or going outside, or playing with other children; or the woman who is afraid of her husband's snobbishness; or the man who is afraid of his wife's nagging—they all can be helped by practicing determination.

It is very important that you make a firm decision. When you are fully one-pointed, that creates willpower. When you make a decision, all the different modifications of the mind come together and create willpower for you. If your mind is dissipated and scattered and flies from one place to another, then you will not have willpower. Decide before you go to bed. You are the doer; do not do that which you think should not be done. Tell yourself, *I am not going to do it tomorrow.* The part of mind that has been motivating you to do it will come forward. *But it is good. Why do you tell me not to do it?* Again you determine, *I will not do it!* When you go to bed, go through the process of building samkalpa-shakti. Decide that you will not do that which you think should not be done. Tell yourself, *I am not going to do it tomorrow. I will not repeat it again. What I do tomorrow I will do efficiently. I will not hurt or injure anybody. I will avoid speaking useless lies because that weakens my willpower.*

But if you repeat the mistake, forgive yourself. If the whole world forgives you, that is nothing. But if you do not forgive yourself, it is constant torture. Perhaps you will stumble again, but don't give up. Sometimes failure is a pillar of success. Pray to the Lord: *Lord of life who is seated beyond body, senses, and mind, you know me. You are witnessing all my thoughts and actions, my Lord of life. Give me the strength and energy so that I can fulfill the mission of life, so that I can go through this journey without any interference, without hurting or harming anyone.* In this way you are coming in direct contact with the source of consciousness and that will give you strength. Muscle strength is nothing; strength of mind is tremendous, but the strength of Atman is immense! Those who depend on the strength of Atman are great.

The second thing Gandhi recommended was prayer. He said, "One should feel that I am a living shrine because Infinity is in me. I am not great; I am merely a shrine. Just as a shrine is made out of bricks, mortar, and other materials, so my body is made up of the five tattwas, the five elements. Inside me dwells His Majesty." If you remember that, you will never be afraid and you will not have bad dreams. You will sleep very deeply and you will wake up refreshed.

First cultivate repentance; then create prayer. Contemplate on the Lord of life. *He is everywhere. Therefore, He is in me too. How can I deny it? How can I say that He who dwells everywhere, who is the greatest of all living beings everywhere, cannot live in me? Am I greater than God? No, I am not. Then He is in me. How is it possible for such a great being to be living in such a small body? That is the beauty. He is great because He lives in the smallest; He lives in the greatest.* The sages realize this, but others do not. Such contemplation will comfort you and improve your sleep.

A short breathing exercise should be the final thing you do before you go to sleep.[3] Then you will not have useless nightmares or dreams; you will have a peaceful and deep sleep. Ordinarily, you go to bed because it is time for you to go, whether you are feeling

[3]See Appendix B, Sleep Exercise.

sleepy or not. You do not know the technique of how to sleep. You want to sleep because it is late, but you toss and turn on the bed and do not get sleep. Your partner is sleeping and you do not want to put the lights on and disturb her or him. You should do this breathing exercise before you go to sleep; it is better than lying awake and allowing your mind to remain active, roaming around and becoming too negative. Breath awareness is good. This should be done after repentance and prayer, just before you sleep.

Do not torture yourself while going to bed. Do not go to sleep with great worldly burdens, cursing your husband. *He does not come home on time. He does not give me enough time because he is so busy. I have committed a mistake in marrying this man.* If you go to sleep with this burden, you will have nightmares, and in the morning you will feel as though someone has beaten you.

You expect too much from life. Life should be taken very lightly, but your duties should be taken very seriously. Enjoy! When you go to bed with many worries do you think that sleep is going to solve your worries? This is not the job of sleep. Do you know that if you weigh yourself with worries, you will weigh less? One who has no worries weighs more. You should not go to bed with the burden of worries. They reduce you in all ways — your capacity, your vitality, your energy, your understanding, and your memory. Tell your worries to come to see you in the morning, not to go to bed with you or trouble you at night, for they will give you bad dreams and disturb your sleep. Worrying is a disease that you have acquired. You have been worrying your whole life and yet you are still alive. If you look at your past, you will find that your whole past was full of worries, but you are still alive and you are smiling. Based on this experience, ask yourself not to be affected by worries. Worrying consumes your energy. Worrying is like a car in motion that is not going anywhere. Your mind is going through the thinking process, but you are not progressing. There are some people who really like to worry. They feel that if they do not have any worries, what is the point of living.

Mind control does not make you inert or desireless. Mind control makes you creative, well balanced, and skillful. It cannot prevent you from worrying, but it can help you to control and modify worries. No one can say they do not have worries, but some people can say, "Yes, I have worries, but I don't allow them to affect me." You cannot enjoy anything if you worry. You cannot enjoy sleep, sex, food, or anything else. You cannot enjoy your very existence. You should learn to enjoy everything by not allowing any worries to affect you. When you have to do something, do it; do not keep it in your mind and worry about it. This is a very bad habit. Hypertension is created by worries. When you go to sleep, be free from all worries.

If you go to bed with a disturbed mind, you will not be able to sleep well. If you eat your food and fight at the dinner table, rest assured that you may be eating good food but you are creating poison internally. If you do sex under pressure, instead of enjoying it you will have a bad experience. When mind is disturbed, your biochemistry changes. It is very important for you to eat food in cheerfulness, to sleep in cheerfulness, to do sex in cheerfulness.

Very few people understand what sex is. There are many aspects of sex: sex as an act, sex as a part of love, sex as lust, sex as a necessity. This is a topic that people don't discuss or try to understand. One can remain easily without sex. It can be suppressed and repressed, but that is not good. By refraining from sex you are not controlling that urge. Why do you give so much importance to the sexual act? It has created a greater impression in your mind because you have put so much value on it. Neither is it good to give too much importance to it, nor to be loose about the sexual act. Sex is one of the primitive urges and it should be understood and regulated. It can hamper your progress if you do not control it. This does not mean becoming fanatical or forcefully restricting yourself from doing sex. If you do that, you will only think about sex more and more. Nature controls the sex life of animals and not of human beings because human beings are more evolved. They have a mind and they can understand what to do and what not to do. For human beings the sexual act is meant to be an expression of love. Sex should be accepted and respected as an expression of love, but the whole expression of love is not only sex. Sex is a part of the expression of that love which is based on equality. It is participation in an act to give comfort to each other. If it is not comfortable, it means there is no understanding. If there is no understanding, it means there is no love. If sex is done without love, then it is no more than masturbation. Sex as an act without love is stressful and can create problems. If you go on doing sex with anybody you meet on the way and you form the habit of jumping from one partner to another, there will be no end to it. You will become sick because it will affect your mind. You may think it is a joy or call it experience. Many such experiences bring sickness. If you do not know what sublimation is or what command and control are, then it is better that you have one sexual partner and that you try to adjust and understand. If a boy and girl are driven by the crazy notion that sex alone is alive, there is a way of disciplining that drive. As two banks discipline the flow of the river, the boy and girl should understand that marriage is also a discipline.

Most marriages are not successful because of sexual incompatibility. Many women nag their husbands for sex. Many men demand so much sex, yet they are not competent. Then, eventually the marriage falls apart, which is creating great havoc in the world. Women say there are only a few real men in the world. Men say that women are frigid. There is nothing wrong with either of them, but they do not understand each other. The man thinks his wife is like a piece of furniture he can sit down on and use anytime. He is rash in the sexual act. He does sex quickly and gets up, and the poor woman suffers. That should not be; there should be an understanding. When the couple cannot adjust in sexual understanding, the marriage falls apart. Sex is understandable; in many marriages there is too much demanding and not enough understanding of what each other is going through. They each have their own points of view. The best way is to create a bridge of understanding. Each partner should understand the other's emotions. If love does not have understanding, then marriage is a great sickness for which there is no medicine and no counseling. Very few people are educated about sex. If you learn to give from the very beginning, then sex will be enjoyable. But if both man and woman learn to take, then who will give? Both will remain unsatisfied. The art of sex is not really known. This is one of the biggest problems the modern world is facing; yet everyone continues making love all the time. Everyone's mind is focused there only.

I am not condemning sex. To do sex or not to do sex is not the question. I would never tell you that you should not do sex. Even if I were to tell you this, you would not listen to me. I am not saying that you should go and live in a monastery and not do sex. I am telling you that doing sex without control or understanding what you are doing is not healthy.

The art of how to do the sexual act should be known: the energy fields, the finer forces of life, and the biorhythms should be understood. The right nostril should be activated before you take food or before you do sex. It takes only a half a minute. This is a practical point and you will find it makes a difference. Never force yourself to do sex or to do sex because of excessive vanity. A man cannot prove himself to be a man by doing sex many times with many women. Theoretically, it is possible for one man to make one million women pregnant. At the same time five men are not able to satisfy one woman. Understand the disparity. A man should know the art of sex so that sex does not create frustration or disappointment. If the man is not able to satisfy the woman, he feels frustrated inside. The woman does not want him to have a complex, so she pretends. She behaves as though she is enjoying the act, though she is not. Neither masturbation in sex without understanding is good, nor is pretending. It's a simple thing: when man becomes active, woman remains passive; when woman becomes active, man becomes passive.

No one should indulge in sexual activity just after a meal. Doing sex after taking food is injurious. You are bound to have some problem, especially with your liver. There should be at least four hours' difference. Doing sex immediately after food also affects the appendix and disturbs its secretion.

You should never do sex in the early hours of the night. The best time is between three and four o'clock in the morning, when you are physically rested and relaxed, and your food has been digested. Untimely sex invites disease.

When two people live together, they should not live only on the level of action. They should also live on the level of thought because it is thought that motivates action. When two people think alike they can live together nicely. If two people think differently, they cannot live together. They can agree and disagree on and off, but not always. Husband and wife should have understanding in all dimensions, such as their worldly goals and their final goal or the purpose of life. They should understand why they are living together, and what they need in the world. They should set their goals in the world, but they should not just live in fantasy, having many worldly wants. They should also have a purpose of life. If two people meet and decide to live together, they cannot be happy if they do not understand why they are living and what the purpose of life is ultimately. If you have attained your worldly goals, what is next? If two people decide to live together and to attain the goal of Ultimate Reality, happiness, and bliss, then all their activities and all that they have in life can be applied for attaining their goal. This is very important. If the final goal or the purpose of life is not known, life becomes very difficult. Husband and wife's relationships cannot be strengthened only on the one level of sexual relationship. Understanding should slowly grow and the purpose of life should be understood. A husband and wife can live together without having any problems if they both are spiritual. It is spirituality that brings husband and wife together. Nothing worldly can bring them together. You should have worldly goals, but you should have a purpose of life and you both should work for that purpose.

Husband and wife should learn how to be selfless. Homes are not meant to radiate selfishness. They are meant to radiate love. If you are not selfless, what do you mean by love? If you really want to love someone, then you have to know how to sacrifice even your own needs. If you learn how to live selflessly, then you can attain that state of joy that is attained in samadhi. You can attain that state of joy at home by enjoying your life, by knowing the purpose of life, by leading your life as an act of worship.

Sex cannot be a means for enlightenment except through the path of tantra in which you become aware of two forces—the male and female principles. Then sex becomes an act between two principles and not between a man and a woman. Tantra is a way of transforming the sexual act into an act of worship. Unfortunately, tantra is rarely understood. In the West tantra means sex, but actually it is not that way. Sex should not become an obstacle in your life. There are scriptures devoted to this subject. That process which becomes difficult for you, which becomes an obstacle for you, which creates a barrier for you—the same obstacle can be removed by using it as a part of worship. Then it becomes a means. When sex is part of worship, then it is no more sex as lust. This is a highly evolved subject where wife and husband do not take each other as woman and man, but they respect each other as the female and male principles. Neither is superior or inferior.

The sex urge should be studied and understood. Both food and sex are essential biological necessities. Food is a necessity of the body first. Sex is a biological necessity, but actually it is in the mind. If it is not in the mind, you will not do sex. Sleep is a necessity of both body and mind. Food affects body first and then mind. Sleep affects mind first and then body. Sex also affects the mind first and then body. Suppose you have gone to sleep and you have dreamed that you have done sex and you wake up. Immediately after waking you cannot actually do sex. But if you dream that you have taken very good food because you were hungry, when you wake up you are not satisfied. You are still hungry! The origin of one dream is food; the origin of the other is sex. If you have done sex in a dream, you cannot do sex immediately after waking up because you were satisfied in your dream. If somebody is hungry and eats food in a dream, and you tell him to take food when he wakes up, he will take it immediately, because his hunger is still there. The food urge works from body to mind; the urge for sex works from mind through emotions. One is from outside to inside; the other is from inside to outside. The two dreams have different origins. When you try to interpret dreams by understanding their origins you can easily understand them. In this context dream interpretation can be helpful, but first you have to understand the origin of emotions.

The sexual urge is very powerful because it involves two people, but the most powerful urge is not sex. When the question of life or death comes, you will choose to protect yourself from death over the sexual act. The most powerful urge is self-preservation. You do not understand why you are afraid all the time. All fears come from one corner—

self-preservation. Everyone has the sense of self-preservation. That is why you are afraid and why you remain under the pressure of fear. You are under the pressure of so many fears, how can you enjoy life? When you overact under that pressure, that is insanity. Consciously or unconsciously you are trying to protect yourself in some way that is not within your physical capacity. This primitive urge diverts your mind toward yourself only. You are insecure and afraid and you do not care whether others live or not. You ignore others and you become self-centered. You should ask yourself a question: *What am I afraid of?*

All fears can be put into two categories: you are not confident that you will achieve something that you want, or you are afraid you might lose what you have. You are afraid and you try to protect yourself without understanding what you are doing. All these fears come: *I might lose something. I might lose my body. I might die. I might not gain what I want. What is going to happen to me? What will happen to me tomorrow? What will happen to me in two years? What will happen when I become old? Perhaps I might become insane.* You identify yourself with the worst that you have known. *What will happen if I meet an accident? What will happen if my wife divorces me? What will happen if my practice does not flourish? What will happen if the economy of the country goes down? What will happen if the whole world crumbles? What will happen if I die?* The moment you get whatever you want, you are afraid of losing what you have gained, afraid of not gaining it again. All this negative thinking goes on. Why are you creating something negative? Why do you not say, *What will happen if I am healthy? What will happen if I am rich? What will happen if I am generous?* Why do you not think that way? Fears, fears,

fears everywhere. Fear is there because of the self-preservation urge. You take food because of self-preservation, but you do not do sex because of self-preservation. That is an entirely different drive. You do not sleep because of self-preservation. That also is a different drive.

It is very dangerous to have fears and to brood on them without examining them. Fear invites danger. Don't forget that. When you are constantly afraid of something you do not realize that you are negatively meditating on that thing and attracting that fear. Many times you think, *What if I meet with an accident? What if I meet with an accident?* You are preparing yourself for an accident and you will meet with it.

I will tell you what happened once when I was taking a bath in the Ganges. After bathing I came back to the bank and while I was wiping my body I was looking toward the sky. I did not know there was a snake beneath me. I was sitting on a small rock and it was coiled around the rock. When I would sit, the snake would coil up; when I would get up, the snake also would rise. Somebody shouted, "Hey! There's a snake beneath you. Don't move." The moment he told me, I ran away and the snake chased me. Actually it was not the snake that chased me. It was my mind. My mind was so fearful that I mentally dragged the snake with me, but I thought the snake was chasing me. When I looked back the snake was there and I kept running.

I was very much afraid of snakes. I had developed that thing in my mind and it made my life impossible. I was very miserable. It became such a deep thing. I was only seventeen or eighteen years of age. There were thousands of people who used to follow me. Wherever I sat down to meditate I would look here and there and instruct others to do the same before I would close my eyes. My students were very proud that their teacher was so alert. I even used to check my pockets. That fear became so strong that I would never open the window in the room where I slept. I would take off my shirt and put it beneath the window so there would be no opening, and I would not sleep until I had turned over the whole bed and had seen every corner.

My master said to himself, "It is of no use. I have taught him many things but it is not helping him." He took me to a place and said, "Early in the morning at three o'clock we will start a particular puja. It will be very helpful for you."

I said, "And for you?"

He said, "If you are helped, I am also helped."

After the puja the flowers that we had used had been put aside in a heap. The next morning he said, "That heap does not look nice. Take it away."

When I went to lift it, there was a cobra sitting in it. I said, "My Lord!"

He said, "Bring it here." He was just ten feet away.

I said, "It's a snake."

He said, "So what? I am here. I won't allow you to die. You have to choose whether you respect your fear or you respect me."

It was so near to my face, one strike and Swami Rama would be finished.

He said, "Bring it to me."

I brought it to him. He said, "Just touch it."

I said, "Not possible." When I was afraid of something, I hated it because of the fear.

He said, "Come on. Touch it."

I said, "Not possible."

He said, "Should I order you to touch it? Nothing is going to happen. I take the responsibility. This is the time to get rid of that fear that you have created in your mind. That is not good, son. I am here. What can that poor creature do? He needs your love."

When I started moving my hand the snake would turn its hood. He said, "Come on. It's nothing. Hold it and bring it to me." I dropped the flowers and held it at a distance.

He said, "Sit down. Put it in your lap." I sat face to face to him and put it on my lap, yet the fear was there. Then he taught me.

He said, "Your finger is very powerful. It can poke your eyes. If you condemn yourself, it can do it. Your teeth are powerful. They can bite your tongue. You have a strong blow. It can hit your jaw. Why do they not do that?"

I said, "Because they are aware that all the limbs belong to only one body."

He said, "Why are you not aware that all creatures belong to only one Lord?"

Then that mania turned into something different. I started picking up snakes and putting them into my pocket. "Another extreme!" he said. "You don't have to become a snake charmer!"

There is a place in Bombay where they take out cobra serum. They have big glass tables to take out the venom and the snakes could not move. I used to pick up the cobras so the people there thought that I had some special mantra. I do not have any special mantra. I am not afraid. I came to know the principle of how powerful the mind is, how you can attract people negatively and positively both, and how you can create animosity in somebody if you think negatively about your enemy again and again. That can be more powerful than loving someone.

You are creating danger for yourself by having fear constantly and by projecting that fear. Never have fear. Most fears are based on your imagination. You imagine something and you are afraid of that thing. Even if that thing does not exist, it can happen because of your suggestion. Fear always invites danger. You should be free from all fears. Your mind creates fear because it identifies itself with the object of your fear. Brooding on fears makes you negative and sad and then you become sick. Because of a strong sense of self-preservation you become insecure, petty, and small-minded. Life can be enjoyed in all situations. When you forget this, you fall into the grooves of your past habits.

You even become dishonest because of your fears. If you have no fear, you will always be honest. You are afraid of what others will think about you, what they will say about you. This is only one side of it! You should also understand how you think and feel about yourself, and how you understand yourself. Only when you have self-confidence will you have confidence in others. If a German shepherd dog knows that you are afraid, it definitely is going to bite you. If the dog knows you are not afraid, he will not bite you.

When I was at a small resort called Bhawali in the Himalayas, one of the British generals there had a pair of Great Danes. I used to do a practice to find out the subtle fragrance that remains dormant. For that I needed flowers, so every morning I would go to the resort and pluck some. I was just thirteen years of age and did not have the sense that it was somebody else's garden. One morning when I was plucking the flowers for my morning puja, that general warned me, "Hey, young swami. This is my garden. Don't trespass. I have dangerous dogs and they will kill you. I will not be responsible. If you trespass again, I will inform the police and you will be arrested."

I said, "Just let me pick the flowers and don't worry about the dogs. I will handle them."

He informed the police that a young swami came every day, plucked flowers, and went away. The police were very kind to me and they just smiled and ignored this. The next morning the general let his dogs loose. When they saw me they started barking and coming toward me. I stood and said, "Don't do this. What have I done to you? All I do is come to pick flowers. You are obeying your foolish master."

They stopped. I whispered something to the dogs and petted them and showed them that I respected them. They both lay down and I took away my flowers.

After that when their master would call them, the dogs wouldn't go to him. I pointed out to him that the dogs wouldn't bark unless I said they could. The next day there was a Rs.25,000 suit filed in the court against me that I was a magician who had hypnotized the dogs and now they had become useless. I did not use hypnosis. If it was indirect hypnosis, then I'm sorry. I did not know.

One of the police officers came quietly at night and said, "You are creating problems. You are trespassing and plucking flowers. This is illegal and you know it."

I said, "Yes, but I want to set this man right. He is too proud and he hurts many people. Every day he gives a report against someone to the police. He harasses everyone. I am the fittest person to fix him. I am going to set him right."

I had to appear in the court. The judge said, "Swami, have you hypnotized the dogs?"

I said, "I do not know dog hypnotism, and I do not hypnotize. I confess that I am guilty of plucking some flowers, and if you want to fine me, I will pay you."

The judge knew me, so he dismissed the case.

I have but one rule in my life. That is called self-confidence. That self-confidence is not built on ego or on having wealth, family, or many friends. Confidence comes from within. Whatever you do, do it in such a way that you are confident of your actions. You can have self-confidence by becoming aware of the immortal Self that is within you. I don't have self-confidence in my body, senses, or mind. I have confidence in my Atman — my soul — and the cosmic soul. Confidence comes when you go to the source that is the immortal part of your being. That which does not have its own existence cannot give you self-confidence. When you know the immortal part of yourself, then you become confident. The more you become aware of the Reality within, the more confident you become. If you are not aware of the Reality within, you will remain ignorant. Self-confidence means having confidence in the real Self of all, the very source of life and light within you.

You are afraid of examining your fears. They have become habitual and are a part of your life so you have never examined them. Fears develop because you don't examine them. Have the courage to examine your fears. You should not try to escape from anything. When you try to escape from the reality, you become disturbed. That creates a fear that leads to insecurity. When you become insecure you isolate yourself. When you start to isolate yourself and create boundaries around yourself, you cannot communicate with anyone. Fear can create a permanent insecurity and become a disease. When you examine your whole life you will come to know that it is fear that obstructs your progress, that hinders your joy, and creates obstacles for you. Why did you get married? You are afraid of living all alone. You are insecure and you want some security. You want to lean on somebody. You worry that your partner might leave you, so you want to have children. Your husband or wife could not give you security, so you think your children will give it to you. After your children, you think your grandchildren will give it to you. Finally you realize that nobody can give you security. The first and foremost thing is to be free from all fears.

How can one be free from fear? What is the way to overcome your fears? Face them and examine them. Most fears are not genuine. When you examine your fears you will come to know that they are not real. If you leave them unexamined, they will grow. Do not allow them to grow. If you cannot examine them independently, go to somebody who can help you do it. You should always encounter your fears. Never leave them as they are. The more fears you have, the more you sow the seeds of disease. The more you explore yourself, the more you will understand about yourself positively, and the more you will gain freedom from the fears that are self-created.

You can give up your house, you can give up the best thing that you own, but your biggest fear is giving up your body. You are afraid of losing your body because of the self-preservation urge. Death is a mystery to the human mind because no one explains what death means. You should have a proper definition of death so that you are free from the fear that is in your heart and mind regarding death. Death never comes again and again; it comes only once. You are born in this lifetime only once and you will die only once. If you remain under the fear of death all the time, you waste your energy and strengthen that fear. This is not helpful for your unfoldment. Death is a part of life; life is not a part of death. Death is a habit of the body. Anyone who is born is sure to die. You forget that you have come to this world only for some time. This is just a station or a camp in the eternal journey. If you forget that this is a camp and keep saying, *This is mine, this is mine*, you create misery for yourself.

You want to be happy but you create problems for yourself. All the problems and conflicts that are within you are self-created. You do not understand the relationship between the external world and the world within. You do not know how to create a bridge, how to understand, how to know the things around you. They affect your inner being so much that you are frightened. You can relate with people, you can smile, you can say that you are very happy, but inside you are a coward. All the time you remain controlled by fear.

Anyone who has lived in the Himalayas or who is living in the Himalayas will be fearless because he has to cope with natural calamities all the time. When I used to live in Uttarkashi deep in the Himalayas I was still young. I lived in a quiet place about four miles away from Uttarkashi. Everybody thought that this man who lives all alone on the mountain is the greatest of all yogis. If somebody remains aloof, people think that he's a great man. But that's not true. Many people use this trick for name and fame. I didn't because from the very beginning I was trained to be quiet and to be alone. Many people learn to be calm and quiet so they remain quite aloof. Some people retreat because they cannot handle the situation in the world. There are both sides. Going away and searching for solitude is not always good. If you don't have any method or any aim, solitude can cripple your life.

Three swamis from the plains had heard about me and they came to the mountains for the first time. There is always a difference between swamis of the plains and swamis of the mountains. Swamis of the mountains are very poor and don't have anything. They don't care because they don't want their peace to be disturbed. Swamis in the plains are just like me these days—wearing nice clothes. In the mountains it doesn't matter. The beard is not cut because there are no scissors and there is no need of shaving. You cook one meal for yourself, enjoy it, and then you are all alone to meditate, write, and live with nature. These three swamis came and said, "Sir, we have come for the first time. Can you take us to Gangotri?"

I said, "This is July, the rainy season. There are avalanches, mud slides, and floods in the Ganges."

There are three seasons in India—winter, summer, and rainy season. Rainy season means rainy season. Summer means summer, and winter means winter. There is no fluctuation here. In the month of July it rains heavily.

"Oh, are you afraid?"

I said, "I'm not thinking about myself. I'm thinking about you and if something happens to you."

"What? Do you think you people are superior to us?"

I said, "Look. In the mountains nobody goes from one place to another during rainy season. That's called *chaturmasya*. For three to four months no one moves from place to place."

They refused to listen and forced me to go. The greatest of all teachers is nature. They were three and I was one. They said, "We need two ponies."

I said, "What for?"

"What will we eat?"

I said, "If you want ponies and rations and all things, then you can go all alone. With me you don't need anything. We will eat whatever we get—some roots or some vegetables. You can carry supplies for one day, but I am sorry I cannot carry anything for myself. You have to climb the mountain and you will be walking like a donkey. What good is that?"

So they arranged for ghee, sugar, dahl, and rice. I said, "I am not going to carry anything."

"Then you won't have anything."

I said, "I don't care. But I am not going to carry anything with me except one kamandalu (pot) and one staff. That's all." I used to wear one blanket. I made a hole in the middle of that blanket and said, "Come on. Let's go."

Nothing happened the first day. They cooked their meals and all that. Swamis are not allowed to cook their meals because if they waste their time for meals, then they are exactly like you. So according to their tradition, they don't. I told them, "Look. I am a swami. I am not allowed to touch the fire or to go near the fire. You cook. If you want to give me something, give it. If you don't want to give me anything, I don't care." They took pity on me. They would eat first and then give to me whatever was left. I agreed. I said, "I won't clean your utensils. Remember this."

So they said, "Suppose we give them to you?"

I said, "I'll throw them in the Ganges."

We would walk ten to fifteen miles a day. The third day we had to cross a road where there were mountain slides. I said, "Look. This is not the time to go. Let's go in the afternoon. In the mountains we walk in the afternoon from three to six p.m. We don't walk in the morning or late in the evening."

"No. We want to go early. Every day you say something else."

"Why did you bring me if you don't listen to me?"

"Oh. Again you are afraid?"

I said, "Okay."

Nature always tests your inner strength. There was an avalanche ahead of us and we could not go ahead. Another avalanche started coming behind us also. That avalanche blocked the way of the Ganges and it became a dam. Slowly the water started swelling. They looked at me and became very angry. I said, "Let's pray to God that we won't be hungry. Nothing else."

They couldn't cook food because there was nothing, only the road. On both sides it was as if thousands of bombs were being thrown. When an avalanche falls it makes a tremendous sound. They started crying. I said, "This is not the first time I have been trapped. This happens to us many times and we have to be patient and wait. If we have to live, we live."

They were very much afraid. One of them said, "We will kill you before we die."

I said, "I have not done it. I told you not to take this venture."

"If you live in the mountains, you should have power. Everyone thinks you are a great swami. What has happened to your swamihood? Can't you stop it?"

I said, "It's nature. You have to be patient."

They were crying helplessly. A human being becomes the poorest of all creatures because of fear. He forgets himself; he forgets the Lord. When I smiled and laughed at them, they would get angry. Many times they lifted rocks to hit me. I said, "Suppose we die? Many worms die."

"Are we worms?"

I said, "Yes, because you are afraid like that."

That day I thought there is no need of becoming a renunciate. Just be what you have to be. One of the messages of the Himalayan sages is fearlessness. If you are not fearless, how can you enjoy your life? You should learn to enjoy all the things you do. Every gesture should be full of enjoyment. If you have fears, you cannot do anything. Religions do not teach this way. In the name of religion preachers create fears in your mind. They completely distort the teachings and create more fear in you. You have to be fearless. You cannot attain the kingdom of the Lord if you have any fears.

Fear is created by ignorance. If you understand the known and unknown parts of life, the relationship between body and mind, and how body and mind are related to the soul, then you will come to know that there is something within you, a center within you, that is fearless. That center gives you peace, happiness, and bliss. Fears go only up to the level of mind and not beyond. When you start receiving glimpses from the unknown part of your life and slowly become aware of the center within from where consciousness is flowing on different levels, then there will be no chance of any fear. Ignorance and fear are one and the same. If you want to see how ignorant you are, collect your fears and put them on the table. When you have no fears you will understand the mysteries of life here and now. You can never be fearless if you are not here and now. To live without fear is to live in perennial joy. Learn to jump in joy all the time. That is not possible without having right knowledge.

Freedom from all fears means freedom from all miseries. If you have really attained freedom from all fears, you have become master of the four fountains. You cannot do that unless you have the right attitudes—attitude while taking food, attitude while sleeping, attitude when doing the sex act or before deciding that you want to do sex, and attitude toward self-preservation. Even if you know how to take food and which food is helpful and healthy, and then how to sleep and how to do sex, if you are doing all these under the pressure of fear, there cannot be any enjoyment in your life. You have come for such a short time in this world, why waste it by hating, hurting, harming, thinking negatively, and behaving as though the burden of the whole world is on your shoulders? You should learn how to enjoy every moment. Even those who have enough objects to enjoy do not enjoy them. Those who have no objects to enjoy, pray for them. Both are unhappy. To have something or not to have something is not the point. To know the art of enjoyment is real life, and for that you have to form the right attitude toward life, and mainly toward the four primitive urges—food, sleep, sex, and self-preservation.

There are two ways of studying this philosophy and practicing this science. One is the monastic way—the path of renunciation. The other is the path of the world or the path of action. This is the path of discipline. If you understand the four primitive fountains, you will understand that it is important for you to discipline yourself. Learn to discipline your eating habits, your sexual habits and your sleep habits. Discipline yourself and do not uselessly have fears. Discipline makes you aware of your energy level and your capacity. Discipline makes you aware of the instrumentation, the power, the resources, and the potentials that you have. Neither extreme is allowed — overdoing things or not doing.

I have some advice for you. I know you will never take it, but it is my duty to give it to you because I am describing Patanjali's system. My advice is not to do anything beyond your capacity. I am not telling you "don't" for anything. Life is not meant for don'ts. Patanjali never said, "Don't do it." He said to do it under conscious control. You should have complete control; it should not affect you. If outside you are very religious, but inside you are thinking about sex, drinking, and dancing all the time, this is not good. Such people suffer and make others suffer. If you are not supposed to do something, then don't do it. It is better to encounter the urge and understand what it is. It is not good to escape. Try to understand it instead of making it taboo. All the urges should be understood. On the yogic path it is important to learn how to sublimate, how to divert the energy, and how to prevent the mind from going to the grooves of the urges. Discipline is important. *Discipline* means "to regulate your appetites, to regulate yourself." There are many yogic methods to help you to regulate the appetites. *To regulate* means "to find your own capacity." It is better to regulate instead of going to the extremes of suppressing or overdoing. When you regulate all your appetites, and you are no longer a slave to your appetites, that is control. You become the master of that thing which controls your life. This is the difference between a yogi and a person who is called a bhogi. One who is a bhogi becomes rogi. *Rogi* means "diseased." One who has controlled the appetites becomes a yogi.

When Patanjali speaks of mind and its modifications, he includes the thoughts, emotions, and all these primitive forces. Even if you only study these four primitive forces, you will be able to progress. There is a technique for knowing how to sleep and how to eat food. Patanjali does not say not to eat food. If the best food is offered to you, can you say you do not want to eat it? If you do not happen to sleep sometimes, can you just go on without sleeping? Do you have that power? *Okay. Today I will not sleep because I have to do some important work. I will sleep later on.* Why are human beings so completely controlled by sex? What is the point of it? Can you abstain from it? Consciously abstaining from sex is control.

There are only four basic urges that are the fountains of the many streams of emotions. If these four fountains are not understood, you cannot analyze your emotions. First, you will have to find the most suitable way to regulate your appetites, and then you will have to understand your emotions. Otherwise, emotional havoc can control your whole life.

You are a Citizen of TWO WORLDS

You are a citizen of two worlds, the world within you and the world outside you. You have to understand both worlds. They are two different things. One is reality; the other is a projection. One is real; the other seems to be real. You have to establish a bridge between these two worlds. It is not possible to remain totally isolated from the external environment, trying to achieve happiness within yourself, nor can you depend solely on the world and society to make you happy. If you are not happy internally, if you are not happy in your home, you cannot be happy outside. Happiness will not come to you by changing homes. If you are not happy in the world, you cannot be happy in the monastery. That is only escape. If you really are serious about working with yourself, you should be neither egotistical and think that you know everything, nor should you be depressed and think that you know nothing. Just start working with yourself and study yourself. First study that part which is apparent, then that part which is latent. Then you can study that part which is beyond. Sometimes you are inspired to study good books and they make you aware that there is something higher in life that you have to attain. But the most interesting book to be studied is the book of life. Other books can only give you some glimpse or inspire you, but the source of knowledge is within you. You have to tap that source which is deep within you. Before you can go to that source you have to pass through many barriers. The first is the barrier of emotions.

You have to understand both the inner and outer worlds. The inner world is the world of thinking; the outer world is the world of expression. You express what you think. Between these two worlds comes that force called emotion. If you study the book of life and how your emotions are working, how you feel, and how you think, you will understand that emotions are different from feelings and from the thinking process, and feelings are different from thinking. You have to deal with yourself on all three levels. Although emotions are quite different from the thinking process, they are generally linked together because they are not properly understood. You all think and you have the capacity of understanding, but that understanding is not more powerful than your feelings and your emotions. You cannot have any emotions without feelings, nor can you think if you do not feel anything. If your body is senseless and you are in deep sleep, and somebody touches your body, you will not feel the touch nor will you know who is touching you. Just as thoughts are important, so emotions and feelings are equally important. You should be very clear in your mind about your emotions, your feelings, and your thinking process. These are three different things.

Emotion is a very delicate thing. Your emotional body is being tossed all the time like a fish in the ocean of life, which is constantly in turmoil. It is very difficult to control emotions, no matter how educated you are. How can you direct the emotional body and control the emotions so they become useful? If you want to analyze your emotions, if you want to help yourself and others, you have to understand the source of your emotions, the source of your feelings, and the source of your thinking process.

There are two types of emotions: the emotions that come from the primitive fountains, and the emotions that come from the external world from sensations. The conscious mind is receiving sensations all the time. When you receive sensations, they immediately go to your brain and your conscious mind, and then to your unconscious mind. The sensations that you receive from the objects of the world are converted or colored by the conscious mind and your thinking process. The conscious mind is like that part of the coffee pot where you put the coffee grounds. When you drink the coffee, you don't drink those grounds. You drink the coffee that has been percolated, that has gone through the process of filtration, and you throw away the grounds. The impressions and sensations that come from the external world are like the coffee grounds. When you receive a sensation, if the conscious mind takes interest in it and does not reject that sensation, it is carried to the unconscious mind where it remains and affects other impressions there. Any sensations that you receive have to go through the filter of the conscious mind, after which they go to the unconscious mind where they become impressions. Emotions come from these impressions. If that emotion is related to food, it will go to the food fountain and remain there. If it is concerning sleep, it will be there. If it is concerning fear, it will be there. If it is concerning sex, it will be there. The sensations that have been received go to their proper places in the unconscious and become motivations and emotions. You live on them, you satisfy them, you work for them. They remain in the unconscious, waiting for the opportunity to be expressed. When the opportunity comes, those emotions become active and surface. When the sensations are received from the external world and after the sensations have become emotions in the unconscious mind, before they are expressed in the external world, they again have to go through the process of filtration by the conscious mind. The emotions and impressions come forward to the conscious mind to motivate you to function in the external world.

The process can be compared to the act of throwing pebbles into a lake. When you throw a pebble into the lake, it creates ripples on the surface and then settles down at the bottom of the lake where it creates another bubble. That bubble rises and bursts on the surface. So one pebble dropped into the lake will create three bubbles. It creates a bubble when you throw it and also when it reaches the bottom of the lake. This bubble comes up and creates another bubble on the surface. You are constantly throwing pebbles from outside into the lake of the mind. The type of sensation you receive in the lake of your mind determines the type of bubble that arises from the bottom of the lake and the type of ripple that is created on the surface. There is a relationship between the sensation received and the impression created by the sensation. Once you have stored the sensation in your unconscious mind, that sensation will create an impression that is similar in quality to the original impression. When it surfaces it again forms a similar impression.

Sense contact with the objects of the world gives you sensations, and when you receive sensations you feel something. Feeling comes into existence when sensations go to the level of the primitive fountains and the emotions coming from there, such as desire, anger, jealousy, pride, egotism, and attachment. Emotions are very powerful, but the primitive urges are stronger and you should try to understand them before you talk of feelings. Feelings give strength to the primitive desires or emotions that are coming out of the primitive desires. Feelings can be compared with a blind man who can walk but does not know which is the right direction to walk. Feelings in their primitive state are very dangerous unless they consult the mind and go through the process of filtration. You may be considered to be a cultured, educated person in society, but suddenly a single emotion upsets you and you start doing things that are not to be done. One emotion can disturb your whole being and turn you into a monster. You may suddenly have an emotional outburst and hurt those for whom you live. Even one who has a sound mind, who is considered to be highly intellectual, can commit a very serious crime in a fit of emotion. It is very dangerous to lose your center in a fit of emotion. Nature controls the instincts of animals, but nature does not control the animal instincts in human beings. Human beings have a mind. When you do not prepare your mind to control your emotions, then you will go to the primitive side and do things that are called crimes. Committing crimes like child molesting and rape is a disease. Such people need to be treated and to have training so they will stop committing crimes. Crime is not just something that one does. It is a disease and it should be treated. When primitive feelings and emotions are not allowed to go through the thinking process, the person cannot discriminate between what is right and what is wrong. He becomes like an animal because animals don't think. When emotions and feelings affect the thinking process, then you start to commit crimes internally. When you do not check your emotions and feelings and you do not allow them to go through the filter of the thinking process, they remain primitive and can control your whole life.

There are three types of actions, thoughts, and emotions. Whether they are negative or positive, actions, thoughts, and emotions can be qualified as mild, medium, or intense. An emotional fit comes and you pick up the rod from your fireplace and hit your husband's head. Or, suddenly emotion comes, the child becomes very cruel and hits his pet and the pet dies. That fit is described as intense. The medium type takes some time to build up. Have you ever eaten pickles? Pickles are made out of vegetables, but you cannot make pickles overnight. It is a long process. When the vegetable goes through a change, it becomes pickled. Medium intensity means negative thinking or brooding over something. *He is a bad man, yes. He talks like this. He is not kind to me.* You are building that up in your mind. There is also another step — mild. You look at the way people are dressed and you frown disapprovingly. I have seen people observing only the superficial garments of others and judging them without looking within. You frown for no reason, and in this manner you increase your wrinkles and nothing else. You form a habit. A mild habit can become medium and then intense. You can watch yourself: the smallest impression that you keep in your unconscious mind can grow stronger. When your interest in the sensation increases, and your actions and thoughts associated with the sensation are repeated over and over, the impressions grow stronger and stronger. A small impression of hatred for someone can gain strength until one day you may even try to kill the person. You can prevent such small impressions from growing by giving positive suggestions to yourself, and by being aware of your progress in life.

If you go on storing all the sensations from the external world, life will become a great burden. As it is life is a burden because you do not know how to handle the sensations that you are receiving all the time. Learn to study your negative actions, emotions, and thoughts when they are mild. Once they become intense, they will drive you crazy and will cause endless misery and ignorance. At Kanpur I once saw a person die suddenly because he heard that he had won the lottery. Previously he was quite healthy and used to jog regularly. He had no problems with his heart. He had bought a seven rupees ticket and he won seven lakhs rupees. He was so happy he died! What kind of happiness was that? It was not happiness. It was intense emotion. He could not control the reaction of the emotion.

You need to understand how your emotions create problems for you and how emotional habits can become a disease. Diseases from different origins are constantly affecting you, and you do not know how to deal with them. There are only a very few diseases that are considered to be purely physical diseases, such as infectious diseases. Physical diseases are simple, no matter how big they are. The mind is involved in most other diseases. Many diseases are mental diseases. Mental diseases are more serious. No matter how much you try, they persist. You may eliminate one disease; another comes. You are suffering because you do not know how to think properly. You are suffering because of your own follies. Emotional diseases are not mental diseases. Emotions can create mental diseases, but they are not mental diseases. Emotional disease is different from mental disease; mental disease is different from nervous disease; and diseases of the brain are entirely different. As far as diseases of the brain are concerned, you cannot do much. When diseases of the brain occur, your mind becomes helpless. You cannot cure brain diseases with mind control.

Psychosomatic diseases come from your emotional body. Psychosomatic diseases are not independently born in the unconscious. They originate in the unconscious, but actually they come from the impressions stored from your relationships in the external world. Any emotion that is creating problems for you, that is a source of psychosomatic disease, is related to someone else. According to yoga science, all emotions have their base outside you. *Emotion* means "relationship." If you want to study your emotions, you should study your relationships and find out what is wrong in your relationships. All of your emotions are related to your family members, your educational institutions, and your environment. Your environment is constantly affecting you. Not a single emotion is your own. Most of the emotions that create problems for you and create havoc in your mind are those that are from the external world. This means you have not understood your relationships with the external world. When you tame the primitive urges, you will be free from those emotions that come up from those urges, but you will not be free from those emotions that come from the external world.

All emotions come from external sensations from the external world, or from the four primitive fountains — food, sex, sleep, and self-preservation —

from which spring seven streams. From these seven streams there are many offshoots, tributaries, and branches. The seven streams are: *kama* (desire), *krodha* (anger), *moha* (attachment), *lobha* (greed), *mada* (pride), *matsarya* (jealousy), and *ahamkara* (egotism). If you understand these streams, you can explain your emotions. If you learn to help yourself, that will be a great help to others because then you will not disturb anyone. Instead of trying to do good in a confused state of mind, it is better not to disturb others. How will you do that? Study the sources of your emotions, from where the emotions spring, and learn how to control your emotions.

The Root Cause of
All Emotions is DESIRE

Life in the external world is important, but life within is even more important because your actions are actually your thoughts. Your thoughts are based on your emotions, and your emotions are virtually your desires. When you desire something, that desire becomes the motivation that moves your whole being. You should understand this principle. The root cause of all emotions is desire. Millions of desires are there in the mind and those desires are creating thought patterns. You have a desire to fulfill, and if your desire is not fulfilled, you become angry. Anger comes about because your desire is not being fulfilled. If it is fulfilled, you become greedy and egotistical. Ego is that I-ness or my-ness that separates you from the whole. You become proud because you have something. Your desire has been fulfilled and someone else's desire has not been fulfilled, so you become proud. Attachment is the cause of misery. You are always afraid that you might not get what you want or that you might lose what you have, so you cling to it. If someone has something you want, you become uselessly jealous. These are the seven main sources of emotions. These seven streams are the products of the four fountains. By properly analyzing your emotions and the origins from which the emotions come, you can help yourself.

Suppose you are angry because you are sexually frustrated or because you could not have what you wanted to eat. These two angers will have two different effects. The first will have a mental effect and the other will have a physical effect. If a child is committing a mistake that is harmful to the child, for disciplining the child you say, "Don't do that." This is not anger. You love the child and you want to discipline the child, so you pretend to be angry, though your anger is under control. If you have that type of anger, then it is good, but if you lose your temper and commit a crime, such anger is not good. When you get angry, your blood pressure goes higher and your nervous system is definitely weakened.

My kung fu teacher was very old — over ninety. I never knew exactly how old because if we asked him his age, he would say, "No age. I am beyond age. Why are you asking?" Practice was the object of his teaching. Practice means experiencing, and ex- periencing means allowing experience to become your guide. If I have been rude to you, I have experienced that it is not good. I should allow this experience of mine to guide me whenever I have the tendency to become rude later on. When you know something you should learn how to practice it. You should allow your past experience to come forward. Suppose in the morning the teacher taught us not to be angry; in the evening he wouldn't say anything but he would make us angry. He would do certain things that we did not like and we would become very angry. Nothing would happen to him. He would smile and say, "In the morning I taught you not to be angry, so it is a fresh teaching. You have forgotten after only a few hours. There must be some weakness in me or in you. Either I am not teaching properly, or you are not practicing properly. Will you just consider who is right and who is wrong?"

Sometimes you claim that you have controlled your anger, but anger can also remain in latent form. A vast part of your personality remains submerged in the unconscious. Anger is a particular desire in modified form. If the desire is not fulfilled, then you get angry. You are constantly feeding your ego—that is why you are angry. You have anger and you are hiding that anger. You are suppressing something in your heart and mind. You hold anger within but outside you smile. You express only your best side and the worst side you suppress. When a friend comes you say, "Hello, how are you?" You are very polite, and people call you civilized. When you get married, you make many promises to your wife, "Oh, I will look after you and you will be the queen of my heart. You will be the angel between the sun and the moon." You say many such things and the poor girl believes you. Once you are married to her it is easy for you. You let out all your anger on your wife because you could not let it out on your mother, your father, or your friends. They would have challenged you. If the woman is weak, she will accept it the first time. *He loves me. I don't know what happened to him. Let me help him. He is an angry man.*

All of that anger was not expressed, so the next day you get angry again. Now the woman becomes a little bit defensive. The third time she says, *Okay, if you behave this way, I will also use my defense mechanism.*

If you understand the sources of emotions, you can easily understand any emotional problem, no matter how hidden the emotions are, and you will not be disturbed. A disturbed person is one who is weak. If someone disturbs you, you are weaker than that person. It is not good for you to get disturbed when somebody else is disturbed because you will be affected by their disease. You can easily be controlled by somebody who is disturbed. When the conscious mind is ruled by undesirable emotions, fantasies, and problems that are constantly coming and going, then you lose control of the conscious mind. Always tell yourself that no matter what happens, you will not allow your mind to be disturbed. Samkalpa-shakti is built through this. If a hypnotist uses suggestion, it is called hypnosis. If autosuggestion is used by a yogi, it is called samkalpa-shakti.

If mind is disturbed, if mind is depressed, or if mind is agitated by emotions, that mind cannot taste cheerfulness. The greatest physician in your life is cheerfulness. If you want to enjoy good health, you should have a friend with you called cheerfulness. Do not allow yourself to be depressed by thought patterns because you are not your thought patterns. Do not allow your thoughts to influence your internal states. Try to maintain cheerfulness.

Once I was speaking to a large crowd in Hamburg, Germany and I told a long joke. I had a very good interpreter. It took me a few minutes to tell the joke, but the interpreter translated in a few seconds and everyone nearly fell off their chairs laughing. I thought, *I have wasted time in learning English, Sanskrit, and other languages. I am going to learn German.* When the lecture was over I asked her, "Tell me. How did you translate such a big joke in a few seconds' time?" She said, "I told them, 'The speaker is telling a long joke. Please laugh.'"

One should maintain that humor. Laugh with your children and your partner. During laughter you remain very happy.

It should be your very nature to smile. You should always have the attitude that no matter what happens you will keep on smiling. The greatest gift a human being has is not life itself. A human being can smile and can laugh. These are two rare gifts. Very few people know how to laugh. Even though society teaches you to greet everyone with a smile, you have to wear a button that says *smile* because it is not coming from within. If a wife and husband who are the best companions cannot laugh between themselves, but they go to the club and others make them laugh, that is not good. I will tell you one story. This is a fact. Once Charlie Chaplin went to a palm reader and asked if there was any way to get cheerfulness and happiness. The palm reader said, "There is a man called Charlie Chaplin. Go see him once in a week and you will easily laugh and smile."

He said, "I am the same unfortunate man."

To laugh for others is very easy, but to keep on smiling requires inner understanding. The very basis of happiness is missing. If you see the same Reality in your wife that you see in yourself, then you will genuinely smile and laugh. Try to see the same Reality that is within you in your friends and in the members of your family. If you cannot see God within yourself, what type of God are you looking for in church? Life and relationship are something reverential, something great. The same Truth that is within you is in others; this attitude is missing in human relationships.

You try to be secure by possessing things. The more possessions you have, the more proud you become and the more insecure you are. Pride is always false. When you collect garbage for the sake of security and yet you are insecure, then where is the remedy?

False pride cannot help you. The walls of your home protect you from heat and cold, but that is all. You cannot expect much else from them. You have false pride because you have become attached to certain things that you own. You are arresting your growth by having false pride.

The mother of all problems is attachment. Actually, things are not yours, but you claim to own them. Instead of making them a means for enlightenment, you get attached to them. Look at the attachment that you create for yourself. Attachment is an expression of lust. You are attached to something because of your selfishness. I am attached to this microphone, but if I know my real relationship with it, then I will not experience any pain because I am just using it. After using it, I will walk out and it will not give me any pain. When I start owning it, I use it less and get more attached to it. Then it becomes a source of constant pain. You can have all the things of the world, but don't be attached to them.

You are attached to the sensual objects of the world and you think that you are in love. You are attached to the things of the world and actually you are in love with yourself. Love is different from attachment. There is a vast difference. In attachment you want to have; in love you want to give. In love you give things without any attachment or bondage. *Nonattachment* means "love;" *attachment* means "bondage." When you are in bondage, you are caught. You create miseries for yourself. In attachment you are miserable all the time; in love you become selfless and you are always happy. Freedom is love. When you learn to love the means that is giving you enlightenment, you gain freedom. Learn to practice love by not being attached to the things you have, and by knowing the method of using them as a means for attaining your goal. When you love, you become selfless and nonattached. You should live nicely by using the things that you have, by loving all and excluding none. Love is an expression of enlightenment.

You become uselessly jealous because someone else has something. Jealousy creates poverty for you. You become very poor when you become jealous and you cripple the potentials within yourself. You do not find the strength within yourself to reject this feeling. It makes you a pauper. Jealousy is a bad quality. It can also lead to insanity.

You all suffer on account of ego. You live within limited boundaries, and you do not progress because of ego problems. You do not know how to train, purify, and polish the ego. You do not know how to use and apply it, so you lose touch with the internal Self, the center of consciousness, and with the external world. You cannot communicate with others and you cannot benefit from the light within, the source of consciousness; there can be no growth or unfoldment. However, ego can be a very helpful instrument. Ego should be used exactly as you use your shoes so that they wear out. Instead, you feed the ego all the time and never use it, just as many people polish their shoes, put them in the cupboard, and never use them. It is like buying a car, polishing it everyday, and not using it. The ego is meant to be used; you cannot live if you do not have ego. You should have ego, but you should know how to use it. Ego can be transformed so that it becomes a means.

The most dangerous trip in this world is called "an ego trip." All other trips are happy. It is very difficult to culture ego. It is a sickness to educate, feed, and live for the ego. When the ego says, *Everything belongs to me*, it is a very bad thing. Here ego is your enemy because it does not allow you to grow. You cannot see through the corridors of life, so you cannot progress and unfold your personality. Ego can be purified, polished, and transformed. It can be used while doing your actions selflessly. You have to remind your ego that this body and this mind are not yours. There is no place for ego if you really want to be cheerful and happy. There is only one function of ego and that is to conduct your daily duties through your mind, action, and speech. From morning till evening you use the word *I, I, I, I*. That which is used most in the world is *I*, and that which is never known is also *I*. You do not know *I*, yet you use it the whole day. If you really understand that *I* that is beyond body, senses, and mind, nothing is impossible. If you constantly identify with your body and your thought patterns, then that *I* gets mingled and you suffer. If you think *I am body*, then you will suffer because body is subject to change, death, and decay. If you understand and identify with that *I* that is the light in the lamp of life, then you will be fearless. There will be no place for fear in your life.

Mind is very close to the soul and uses the power of the soul. If you put one end of a big bar of steel into the fire, you will find the other end also becomes heated. That heat which comes from the soul is not being utilized properly by the mind because of bad habits. You must learn to help yourself and to purify your mind in order to make the mind aware that this is not your power; this is the power of the soul. Then you will be free from ego problems. Instead, whatever you do, you are always trying to satisfy your ego. All these worships of yours, all these so-called loves and attachments in life, are just food for your ego. Whatever you decide, good or bad, you decide according to your own convenience. You decide for yourself. You love your wife because she loves you. If she does not love you, you are never going to love her, even if she is in bad health. You love her because you are identifying yourself with her. Whenever you identify yourself with someone, you love that person. Watch and see how selfless you are when you are doing some service. You do not do any service without some selfish reason, even though you say you are doing it selflessly. You are doing it either because you want a reward for it or you want to be praised. If these thoughts are not there, then your act is a purely selfless act and your ego will not make you conceited. Selflessness means you are delighted in doing something for others without expecting anything in return. The world has very little to give and you are expecting too much. The world is a mirror. Don't expect too much from a mirror. A mirror only gives a reflection of what you are. That which you can get from yourself, you expect from others; that which you get from others, you expect from yourself. This is the case with relationships. You expect too much from your children, but they have no capacity to give what you expect. A husband expects too much from his wife; a wife expects too much from her husband. Neither has that much capacity. It is better not to expect and to live happily. You expect too much from your teacher and you are not listening because so much expectation is there. Learn not to expect and just act; you will enjoy life more.

The whole world is moved by ego. You are worshipping your ego in the name of God and you say you are worshipping God. When you are praying, to whom are you praying? To ego. For whom? For ego. Why are you eating? For ego. You always say, "*I* do this, *I* do this." From morning until evening you are strengthening ego, and ego has separated you from the whole. Ego becomes stronger and stronger when ego is not aware of another higher existence. As long as you are not aware of the Reality, you think you are everything. That is ego. Ego separates you from the whole and does not help you in going beyond. Ego gives you some flashes of knowledge, but only within the boundaries it has built for itself.

Ego has two sides — higher and lower. The moment ego helps you to go beyond, it is called higher ego. That ego which limits you, which builds a boundary around you that separates you from the whole and does not allow you to be exposed to the higher levels of consciousness, is the lower ego. You can easily understand how you are separated from the whole. If you feel yourself separate as you are, then it means you cannot do anything at all. If you can do something, and you can transform your personality, does it mean that God has not had any part in your creation? Are you created by God the way you are, or can you change and transform your personality? There is something wrong in your understanding. You do not see the solution because mind is a small ruler and you are trying to measure the whole universe with that small ruler. When mind cannot give you the solution the remedy is to go beyond intellect. You have to surrender the ego, which is very difficult. You should not surrender your ego before other human beings. You cannot have faith or surrender your ego unless you have understood the reality of the unknown. Ego can be surrendered to the unknown, to the Reality, to the center of Truth and awareness. When you say, *I belong to Thee. Let me serve Thee with all my might, with mind, action, and speech, without any selfishness,* then ego is helpful. Surrendering ego means accepting higher Reality or awareness. Surrendering does not mean that you are just renouncing your ego. No one is telling you to renounce your ego. Surrendering ego means becoming constantly aware of the Reality that is within. Then you will no longer separate yourself from the whole. If ego can separate you from the whole, ego can also connect you to the whole, if it is properly polished, and if it is made aware of the Reality. If you do not have an ego problem, you will never become negatively emotional or proud and you will never want to possess anything that does not belong to you. When you learn to expand your individual ego to a higher consciousness, when ego goes to a level of higher consciousness, then it becomes an instrument to make you aware of the Reality outside your boundary, and it is higher ego. Then, you say, *I am Thine and Thou art mine. I acknowledge that my existence is because of You.*

When Hanuman crossed the ocean and came back, Rama asked him, "Hanuman, how did you cross the ocean? It is not possible for anyone to cross the ocean. That island is full of evil people and they are very strong. How could you go there and receive all the information about Sita and come back?"

Hanuman explained, "I jumped like this and I jumped like this."

Everybody was surprised that he was being egotistical. Then he said, "This is all because of your greatness."

Ego should not be enveloped with pride but with surrender so that ego shines. That is why yogis say the highest ego is to surrender the ego. *Surrendering* means "becoming aware of the Reality." Let ego remain aware that it is only an agent, not the proprietor. When you allow ego to become your proprietor, you are gone. Ego contracts your personality and separates you from the whole. It does not allow you to grow or to become one with the Reality. That is why the shortest cut is just to cut the ego, and you are *there*.

When I was eighteen or nineteen years old I thought, "I do not need anymore practice. I am perfect. I do not need any teachers or anymore studying. You have taught me everything and I know everything. I am a perfect swami. There is no other perfect swami in India." When I told this to my master, he looked at me and said, "What has happened to you? Are you drugged? What do you mean?"

I said, "No. This is the truth."

After three or four days he said, "I will give you a practice now. You have not understood anything as yet. You have to kill four enemies of yours."

I said, "You teach me nonviolence and now you are ordering me to kill."

He said, "No. This is not actual killing. Remember four things: kama means desire, lust. Selfish desire is the mother of all problems. Have the desire to meet God, but no desire to acquire things for yourself, and no selfishness. Abandon that desire which is followed by selfishness. Second, you get angry. I do everything for you and you do nothing, and yet you get angry with me. Anger means unfulfilled desire. You have a desire to fulfill and I am an obstacle for you, so you cannot fulfill your desire. That's why you are angry. Next is pride. What do you have that you are proud of?"

I said, "I am handsome and healthy and young."

"Are you proud of this?"

I told him many things and he laughed at me.

"Have you read history? What happened to such and such great warrior? Where is he today? People made a tomb for him and where is that tomb? Go and see. You will find donkeys roaming around there. There is no trace of those heroes today. And you are proud. What do you have? What are you proud of? Can you create another little Bhole?" He used to call me Bhole. That was my nickname.

I said, "No."

He said, "Find out what is that thing—you have done something, you have gained something, that you have, that you possess." He made me understand that I don't have anything so I should not be proud.

"Moha is another. Moha means attachment. You are attached to your body though body is not yours. You think it is yours. You are attached to it and you say, 'I am this, and I am this, and I am this.' How can you claim that this body is yours? Can you create another body like that? I taught you to walk straight and you show off. I didn't teach you for that purpose. You are feeding your ego. You are afraid of not attaining what you want and of losing what you have. Because of that fear you do silly things. Okay, kill all these evils and then come to me. You have to do it in six months' time because you are grownup and you should learn to teach others. You have not done anything so far."

I said, "I have learned how to meditate. I can sit for a long time."

He said, "Yes, I know. Have no desires, no anger, no pride, and no attachment. Follow these four guidelines for two months and go to see four swamis. But remember that you are in search of sages. Don't project yourself and your feelings." They were his friends, so he did not inform them that I was coming.

First, I went to see a swami who was very famous for his silence. No matter what happened, he never looked at anyone. He did not have anything but he was very content.

He was sitting on a hillock under a tree. Down below there was a lake. People used to make a fire next to him. He never wore anything in any season so his skin was exactly like elephant skin—weatherproof. All around him were the husks of sugar cane. Whenever he was hungry he would chew those husks. And he was very fat. When I went to him I touched his feet and started pressing them. I thought he would be pleased. Next minute he kicked me and I rolled down five hundred feet to the lake. It hurt me all over. I was angry and I said, "He had no business to do this. Okay. If you kick me once, I will kick you twice. Let me go up."

I composed myself and then I started to kick him. I forgot that I had to kill my anger. Suddenly he said, "You have been asked to kill four enemies and you have not yet killed one. Your guru told you not to get angry. Sit down; I kicked you just to examine your anger. Why are you angry? I did not kick you; I kicked your ego. You should understand this. This kick should remind you that you have to get rid of anger. Why did you touch my feet? Why did you not touch my heart? If you want to know the reason, I will tell you."

Then he said a beautiful thing. "A sage surrenders the best part of his life at the lotus feet of the Lord. People usually recognize you only from your face. If you have given your head to the Lord, the world will never recognize you. If your face is missing, nobody can recognize you. They can touch your feet or your body, but they do not know who you are because your head is somewhere else. Worldly people never recognize those who have given their heads to the Lord. How can the world bother them? They cannot see the face of a sage because it is not there. The best part of a sage is at the feet of the Lord. People find only the feet, so they touch the feet. You should try to understand what is there. Now, you cannot stay here."

I had to leave. I wept because I felt sorry for myself. A few days earlier I had thought that I was a perfect swami. He made me aware that really I was not.

I went to another swami. He knew that I was coming so he left some gold coins at a small fountain in the mountain where we used to go to bathe. Before I went to him I found those gold coins. It came into my mind that I should pick them up, so I picked them up and put them in my pocket. Suddenly I thought, *These gold coins are not mine. Why do I need them? I do not think you are practicing your swamihood.* I put them back. When I went to the swami, he was very annoyed. I bowed before him. His face was long, and he said, "Why did you pick up the gold coins and put them in your pocket? You still have greed. Get out. This is not the place for you."

I said, "But I left them there."

"You left them later on. Why did you pick them up and put them in your pocket?"

I examined myself and realized that I still had much to learn about the latent part of myself.

There are FIVE CATEGORIES of Thought Patterns; Some are Helpful, and Some are Disturbing

Patanjali says there are five categories of thought patterns or modifications of the mind. *Vrittayah panchatayyah klishtaklishta.* These are further characterized into two types — *klishta* and *aklishta* — that which is helpful and that which is disturbing. The five categories are: *pramana* (right knowledge), *viparyaya* (wrong knowledge), *vikalpa* (fantasy), *nidra* (sleep), and *smriti* (memory). Some of these are helpful and some of them are a source of constant disturbance. A good thought comes into your mind. *I should meditate.* This is helpful. Another thought comes. *I would rather sleep. What good is this meditation?* Lazy! *Okay. I'm so young. I will do meditation after fifteen or twenty years when I become old.* Excuse! You will have to understand which particular thought form is helpful and which is not; which is a source of disturbance and which is a source of progress for you.

Right knowledge is that knowledge that helps you to dispel the darkness of ignorance. Right knowledge is that knowledge which helps you to know things as they are, in their totality. Here is another definition: If you only know a part of mind, that is not right knowledge because you do not know mind in its totality. So, *right knowledge* means "knowing mind in its totality."

Right knowledge is called pramana because it is based on facts. That which stands with the help of evidence is called pramana. There are three kinds of pramanas: direct experience; knowledge from the scriptures, or testimony; and inference. If smoke is visible far away in the mountains, you can assume that there is fire because smoke is one of the evidences of fire. If you see smoke just beyond the mountain, even though you do not see fire, the smoke tells you that there is fire. If you know with the help of one of these three pramanas or evidences, that is right knowledge.

How can you gain right knowledge of anything? When you directly experience or perceive something and that is confirmed by the authorities of the scriptures, that is called pramana. In the mundane world, right knowledge is that knowledge which is supported by one of three evidences. Direct evidence: I see that this is a blackboard. I do not need to read the scriptures to help me in knowing that this is a blackboard because I perceive it directly. There is no hindrance to my perception so I can say it is right knowledge. If I cannot prove that this is a blackboard, if I am still doubtful, or if you are confusing me by telling me that this is not a blackboard, then I will study that part of the scriptures that will help me to know that this is a blackboard. I will also look for the symptoms. After collecting all the evidence, I know that this is a blackboard. This is called right knowledge.

When you do not see something in its proper form, and you cannot give any definite name to it, then it is wrong knowledge, or viparyaya. Wrong knowledge is that knowledge that is not supported by anything. If I'm thirsty while driving a car in a desert and I think I see water, but when I go there, there is no water, this is wrong knowledge. A mirage is viparyaya. There is some substance in your mind and on the basis of that substance you see water. Distorted knowledge is viparyaya. Many people do not understand the difference between viparyaya and fantasy. You know what a snake looks like. If you see a rope in the darkness and take it to be a snake, that is viparyaya. Viparyaya is that knowledge that is based on some substance, though it is not right knowledge. Fantasy is entirely different. Fantasy is the creation of a crazy mind.

There is very little difference between fancy and fantasy. Fancy is imagination. Imagination is having an image within. If I have a small harp and a chain, I can imagine a bigger harp that is more melodious. Imagination cannot be called fantasy. You cannot condemn all imagination because imagination can be creative too. What is the difference between imagination and fantasy? How do you fantasize things? I will give you an example. Here is a fantasy: *I am very much angry with the Lord of gods. What shall I do? How can I fight? I have no means. I met a woman who is barren. I went to the son of that barren woman and I asked him to fight on my behalf and he got ready. Then I picked up the bow and arrows made out of donkey's horns and I handed them over to him. He flew far away, crossed all the levels of the sky and galaxies, and went to the Lord of all gods. He killed him and then came back to me.* This is all fantasy. There cannot be a son of a barren woman. There cannot be horns of a donkey, so you cannot make a bow and arrow out of donkey's horns. When the son was not born out of a barren woman, how could he fly and kill? This is called to fantasize.

Fantasy is purely a creation of mind. It is not related to anything.

You should not allow your mind to flow toward fantasy. If your mind goes on fantasizing everything, then your mind will form that habit. Fancy and fantasy are two products of an idle mind. I don't have time to fantasize. I can do that better than you, but I don't have time. I have to do so much work that I wonder if I will be able to complete it. I cannot take rest or eat well because I have to do it. If you make a schedule for your life, you won't have time to fantasize. Just as young boys and girls fantasize, so also in old age the mind becomes preoccupied with fantasies. These are vrittis of the mind and they are not helpful. Sleep and memory can also be injurious if you do not have control over them.

Actually, sleep is one of the states of mind — waking, dreaming, and sleeping. Sleep is not a modification of chitta according to philosophy. Patanjali, being very practical, wants you to understand that as you are trying to control the other modifications of the mind, you should also bring sleep under your control. Patanjali says that anything that is to be brought under your control is a vritti, and you should accept it as a vritti from a practical viewpoint. Patanjali never said that the waking state could be controlled. He is talking about sleep in particular. That which is enveloped with sloth and laziness is called sleep. When you are fast asleep you forget things completely. Though you sleep everyday, you are not aware during sleep. You become unconscious of the facts because your conscious mind does not function during sleep. When it does not function, you do not perceive things at all. During deep sleep there are no contents in the mind. If you are away from the world of facts, and if your senses, which help you in relating with the external world, do not function in the external world, then mind should work within. That does not happen during sleep. Mind also does not relate to your memory during sleep. Before you go to sleep, you become drowsy, your conscious mind starts fading, and you see things in a distorted form. Once I wanted to know how sleep comes, and I could not sleep. For three days I remained well alert because I wanted to watch what happens when sleep comes, but sleep wouldn't come.

Sleep can be compared to death. Sleep is called *sahodari*, the sister of death. Just as sleep relieves us from many pressures, death also gives us rest. Death is a long sleep, and sleep is a small death. You sleep for eight hours. In death you sleep for one hundred hours, one hundred days, one hundred months, or one hundred years. Death is a long, deep rest. After sleep you wake up; death means you do not wake up again. That is the difference.

There are four types of sleep. The first is ordinary sleep. You go to sleep when you are very tired, and you wake up tired. Rest should make your face very soft, but when you get up in the morning, your face looks as if you have not taken rest. It means you have not had sound sleep. You don't want to have disturbed sleep, but you are disturbed. Who disturbs you when you are taking sleep? A part of you wants to sleep, another part disturbs you.

The second type of sleep is *shvan-nidra* (dog nap). That also can be practiced. The way a dog takes a nap is very interesting. Dogs always nap; they never sleep. That nap is sufficient because it is so deep that during that period the dog's brain is creating one hundred percent delta waves, a definite sign of deep sleep. If you make a noise just after the dog falls asleep, the dog will look here and there. Again, after a second's time, he will go back to delta waves. Human beings cannot do that, but you can practice that sleep called dog nap. It is a very useful thing. You can have it ten to twenty times a day, just for a minute. Whenever you get time you can relax and sleep.

The third type of sleep is called sleepless sleep, which is deep meditation or samadhi. There are people whom I have met who claim they do not sleep at all. They do not need sleep. They say that if you know the art of relaxed action, the way of giving yourself rest when you are active, you do not need sleep.

Though sleep is not normally under your control, there is a voluntary way of sleeping in which you can sleep anywhere you like and whenever you want. This is the fourth type of sleep, yoga-nidra, or conscious, controlled sleep. When you wake up after ordinary sleep you say that you enjoyed good sleep because you were not disturbed. Actually, you were sleeping, so you only know that you enjoyed good sleep because you were not disturbed. In yoga-nidra you can sleep and yet you can consciously enjoy your sleep.

Conscious or yogic sleep is the finest way of sleeping. I used to envy some of my teachers who slept for one or two hours, even though they worked very hard. It is possible to learn this method of how to sleep, but the key point is not the unconscious mind. The key point is the conscious mind. If you understand it properly, you can go to a conscious state of sleep and give conscious rest to the mind. This practice does not take much time. It is not something very advanced that you have to become a swami to learn it or leave your home. You sleep every day. In yoga-nidra you will get the most complete rest that sleep can give, and it will be under your control. When you want to sleep you can sleep; when you do not want to sleep you will not. The time to sleep is different than the time to practice yoga-nidra. You are habitually trained to go to sleep at a certain time. Do not use those times for yoga-nidra. Practice yoga-nidra separately at another time. You will be able to do it within one month's time, and you can train others.

When I was young I said, *Let me examine this technique to see if these scriptures are false. If so, then I will tell them it is of no use telling such stories and creating problems for us.* I started learning the method of conscious sleep. Now, if I am fast asleep and people are talking around me, even if someone is talking in Hebrew and I do not understand what they are saying, I can recall it. For half an hour, no matter what you say to me while I am in conscious sleep, I can repeat it back to you exactly as you said it. I can record things better in deep sleep than in the waking state. I trained myself and then had it verified by scientists in order to find out how to educate others.[4] Mind has immense potentials.

One who knows how to control sleep is a yogi. If one does not bring sleep under control, he is not a yogi. Yogis practice the technique of yoga-nidra to bring sleep under control. They go into a state of meditation and consciously control the functioning of the conscious mind, and then they take full rest. While taking complete rest, they remain fully conscious. They are aware of everything going on around them. Such people can maintain awareness

[4]See Appendix A, Sleep.

at an unconscious level when the conscious mind fails to function while leaving the body. They practice yoga-nidra while leaving the body so that awareness does not fail. During death the conscious mind fails and the unconscious mind becomes the vehicle for the soul to travel to the subtler realms. I have seen yogis leaving their body in a fully conscious state. That which they experience during death, they experience every day itself. By having control and knowing the art of sleep they can even control that which is called death.

In our tradition the first thing that is taught in our monastery is the technique of conscious death — how to drop the body and come back again. For a yogi, leaving the body is a voluntary gesture. It is not like death in which a disease comes and troubles you, and then takes away your body. We don't use the word *death* for the process of voluntarily leaving the body. We call it *maha-samadhi. Maha* means "great." It is a voluntary thing that a yogi can do after having progressed and attained the highest state of samadhi. This is the technique of death — learning how to die. Ordinary people do not understand this. You build hospitals for births, but you are thrown in morgues after death for there is no other arrangement. Just as birth needs many arrangements, preparation should also be done for death. The yogis who understand that body is like a garment, cast off this garment silently, without any pain or discomfort, when it is no longer useful. The day humanity understands both birth and death there will be less pain.

There was a swami whose name was Vinaya Maharaj who used to observe silence. He was a great teacher and a very practical man. I was sixteen years of age when I met him. He was completely nude, going toward the Himalayas. It was winter and one of his fingers was in a certain position and he was gesturing. I was coming from the other direction so I looked at him and stood in front of him to stop him. I greeted him and I said, "What is this gesture you are making?"

He said, "This gesture shows that there is only one Absolute without any second. This gesture is not for me; it is to remind others. All the gestures you make are not for yourself; they are for others."

I started to love that person. Wherever he walked he kept making the same gesture. Whenever he sat down he would close his eyes and go into a deep state of meditation. He didn't have anything, not even a pot of water or anything to wear. He used to walk completely nude on the banks of the Ganges. There were no people there except for a few swamis, those who travel and meet each other.

At Allahabad where the Kumbha Mela was going on those days, he said, "I invite you to witness my samadhi."

Because he was a disciple of my master I said, "Should I arrange anything?"

He said, "I want you to witness and to see that I am not troubled by other people. At exactly 4:30 in the morning I will attain samadhi. You should record it for the sake of students."

In our tradition, at least five people should witness maha-samadhi and then the names of the witnesses and how it occurred are recorded in the monastic scriptures. I was there at 3:30 along with four other people. He sat down and we started discussing *Vedanta* and the *Yoga Sutras*. This swami who always used to remain in silence said, "Ask any question."

He would answer the questions in the right way, sometimes laughing. There was no sign that he was about to leave his body. At exactly the appointed time he said, "I wish you good luck. Let you all enjoy the highest state and one day follow the same thing. Om."

And he left his body, just as you throw away a garment that is no longer useful or instrumental in your life. The fortunate few are those to whom the mysteries of death and birth have been revealed. He was one of them.

There is a difference between sleep and dreaming. Dreaming is an intermediate state between waking and sleeping. It is like a passage through which you go to a deeper state of rest called sleep. Some ideas from the objective world and some impressions from the unconscious world are both mingling when your conscious mind gets rest. That state is the dreaming state. I have done much work on mind and dreams. I have been trying to study them from various points of view to find out how to help others.

Sleep can be determined but dreams cannot be. If you want to dream about your boyfriend today, you cannot do that. You will not sleep, and when you cannot sleep you cannot dream. Try it. When you think of your boyfriend for some time, and then keep yourself busy somewhere else, the impression that you have stored in your unconscious mind can come forward as a dream. As long as you remain conscious of something, you cannot dream of that thing.

By interpreting a dream you can know something about that dream, but you have millions of impressions stored in your unconscious mind. Today you dream of something, tomorrow you dream of a different thing, and the day after you dream of something else. It is not necessary for you to know the reason of your dreams. Many times an impression comes from the latent part of your unconscious mind and then you dream it. All the dreams cannot be put in a line for classification. Sometimes you can have a prophetic dream and other times you can have a dream of a different nature. Sometimes you will have a dream of the same type or nature repeatedly. Your fears and anxieties can cause you to keep having the same dream.

Dreaming is necessary for a sick person, but not for a very healthy person. For a sick person, dreaming serves as an outlet for emotions. If he were allowed to do what he wanted, then there would be chaos in society. It is better that dreaming helps him to let out those crazy emotions. For a very healthy person, one who has understood what the waking, dreaming, and sleeping states are, it is a sheer waste of time. You want to sleep and instead you are getting dreams. For a person who has suppressed emotions, the dreaming state helps in letting out those emotions that are not composed in daily life. I hardly ever find myself dreaming because I sleep very little. I have little time so I do not have time to dream.

Dreaming can reveal symptoms about your hidden personality. Hidden desires that cannot be fulfilled in the waking state try to fulfill themselves through dreams. Dreams tell you the qualities of your thoughts, of your inner character, of your past. By examining your dreams you can examine one of the levels of your inner being. You can go through that dream imagery in the waking state and help yourself by watching the natural process of your thinking. Some dreams you remember and some you do not. The dreams you remember sometimes come from gastric problems, such as the bad habit of overeating late at night.

You can try to help people while they are fast asleep — when the conscious mind is sleeping. If your partner is obstinate and has emotional problems, you can talk to your partner when she or he is in deep sleep and you will find that they receive all your thought forms. You can even communicate with a person who is far away from you during sleep. To do this, you should be fully conscious. It is possible for

you to give a dream to your friend no matter where
he is. I have examined this many times. It will only
happen with people whom you know, not with
strangers. It will not work as long as the other person
is conscious, but it will definitely work when they are
fast asleep and the conscious mind is quieted. During
that period you can send your thought forms, and it
is very easy for him to receive your thought forms
when his mind is in a calmer state. If you sit down at
two o'clock in the morning and send your thought
forms to someone, initially his sleep will be disturbed.
If you do it again and again, he will have a dream. I
am not teaching on the basis of what I have read in
books or in the writings of other people; I am teaching
on the basis of self-experience and the knowledge in
the scriptures that have been written by those people
who have really practiced and devoted their time to
the subject.

Sleep learning has been proven to be very useful.
When children are fast asleep and the conscious mind
has calmed down, you can send thought forms to them
for their improvement and you can teach them.
Mentally retarded children, and especially those
children whose conscious mind is not trained and does
not communicate with the unconscious mind, can be
helped. We can read about this in the Mahabharata.

Arjuna, the great warrior of the battle of the
Mahabharata, was married. When his wife

was pregnant he used to come back from the battlefield and give her company. He would always discuss the techniques of battle. She never wanted to listen to this. He said, "Listen. You are pregnant. While I am telling you these things, our child is being educated. Please listen to me. I am telling you the technique of fighting so that my child learns."

She asked, "How is that possible?"

He said, "Note down what I am telling you." He described a technique of how to form a fort so that the enemy could not attack. He wanted to explain how to destroy the fort of the enemy but he could not complete it because by that time she had fallen asleep. At the age of twelve years their child, Abhimanyu, could easily create a fort that the enemy could not destroy. He knew how to do this because of the subtle samskaras that were formed through his mother when he was in the womb.

From the first day of pregnancy you can educate your child. When you are pregnant you should not think in a negative way, you should not be depressed, and you should not become emotional, because all these problems will affect the child. There is a definite way of educating the child, even in the mother's womb.

Smriti means "memory." You should understand the process of memory and how you remember.
First, you see something. Through the contact of that
particular object and your sense of sight you receive a
sensation; you see it. The object that is touched by
your sight gives you a sensation and that sensation
goes through your optic nerve to your brain. When
your conscious mind receives it, then it filters down
to your unconscious to the bed of memory from where
you can recall it. Perhaps, for example, my eyes are
seeing you today and the sensation is being received.
That sensation is very powerful. It contains all the
form and details about you. When I see you, the optic
nerve takes the impression or sensation to my brain
through the channels of the nervous system. As the
original sensation has a form, the impression of your
form that I perceive through my senses is put into my
conscious mind, from which it filters into my
unconscious, where it is left in the storehouse of
memory. If there is something wrong somewhere in
the nervous system, then I cannot memorize your
form. When I see you again after some time I
remember that I have seen you before because the
impression was stored in the unconscious mind. All
thought forms are like that in the unconscious. If I
want to recall a sensation, and I know how to recall it
from the bed of memory, I can tell you exactly that
you were sitting on a certain day, at a certain time, in
a certain row, wearing certain clothes, in a particular
position.

Memory can be categorized as helpful and
unhelpful. Sometimes you memorize something that
is not at all helpful. While you are remembering your
mantra a movie song is repeating in your mind. You
are chanting something different. Memory should also

be controlled. If your memory is not under your control, it will not help you when you need it. You should not say, "I have a friend but I have forgotten her name." Or, "I have read this book but I do not remember it." "Oh, the other day I memorized it but I have completely forgotten it." You study the whole year and finally when you start writing your exam paper your memory does not help you. You keep your conscious mind, the part of mind that you use in your daily life, very busy. Many times you knowingly and consciously put an object somewhere and then you forget. You forget because at that time your mind thinks that it is not important. When it becomes important again, you become tense and confused and then you create a block for your memory. Suppose you have lost your keys. If you worry and make your mind very active to find the keys, you cannot remember. When you are trying to remember where your keys are you fight with yourself and exert your mind. You confuse your mind and lose touch with the bed of memory. By straining your mind you do not allow your memory to spontaneously flow to your conscious mind. If you would relax, you would remember where your keys are. Whenever you are in such a situation, people say, "Just relax. We will find them." You go to the bathroom and suddenly you remember where you put your keys. Most of the things that you forget, you remember in the bathroom. This does not mean the bathroom is the best place for memory, but that you become relaxed there because you are releasing wastes from your system. Toxins that are retained in the body can disturb memory. The more you release the toxins, the better your memory will be and the more relaxed you will be. The best way to know is just to know. Don't fight with yourself or strain. Concentration does not mean straining. There is a process. When you go with that process then you are fit enough to concentrate. You have difficulty concentrating because you are confused and you are not prepared. You have not educated yourself but you are trying to concentrate, so you will be confused and you will strain more and more.

You forget superficial things, but you do not forget the deep samskaras or impressions. If you know ten languages, which is your real language? Even if you can equally read, speak, and write ten languages, the language in which you dream is your language.

Why do you lose your memory? There are two childhoods in our lives. In the first childhood you learn very easily, but if you tell me to take high school examinations today, I would fail. It would be very difficult for me to study the same subjects like algebra and geometry again. Even the professors would fail if they were to appear for the exams. There is a second childhood called old age. That childhood is full of follies. When mind becomes preoccupied, then mind needs unlearning. In the first childhood what is needed is called learning, but in the second childhood unlearning is necessary. The second childhood is a childhood of follies. Elderly persons' thoughts and minds become preoccupied, so they slowly lose touch with their memory. A child's mind is not preoccupied so he does not lose his memory.

Memory means "interest." When you lose interest in something you forget it. Your mind is so preoccupied that you have forgotten what you wanted to do now. You should learn not to be preoccupied. If you learn to let go, then your mind will not remain preoccupied and you will have control over your memory. You have to learn how to organize your mind. Anything that you want to do you can do in a better way by understanding how your mind is functioning and how to use your mind in the best way.

Memory is different from recollection. When I want to recall you, I can recall you from my unconscious. Recollection of thought is remembering, not memory. To know means to just allow yourself to know, to allow your memory to flow to your conscious mind. There are many ways of improving your memory. If memory has come under your control, you will never forget. Whenever you want to recall the stored impressions you can. There is a process for strengthening memory—a simple exercise that I will teach you.[5] There is also a different method that is visualization.[6]

[5] See Appendix B, Counting Exercise for Memory.
[6] See Appendix B, Visualization for Memory.

Your ESSENTIAL NATURE
is Peace, Happiness, and Bliss

The kingdom of God is within. Do not aspire to go to heaven after death. Establish that heaven here and now within yourself. This will happen when you understand the various aspects of your chitta and you discipline yourself. The third sutra states, *tada drashtuh sva-rupe'vasthanam.* When you have control over mind and its modifications you will become a seer and you will be established in your own essential nature. You will no longer be a mere student. You were a student before you accepted the discipline. After you have accepted the discipline and have attained, you will become a seer. A seer is one who sees things as they are and does not get involved with the seen. A seer does not identify with the objects of the mind. You will not be tossed by external stimuli, by the charms and temptations of the world. You will witness things without being disturbed. If your neighbor dies, you will go to the neighbor's home and cry because the neighbor is crying and wants sympathy from you. You will also show your sympathy, but inside you will not be affected because you will know what death means. You will no longer be a simple, confused person who identifies with the objects of the world. You will see and enjoy the things of the world as they are and you will be established in your true nature.

What is your true nature today? You don't know. I am the son of such and such person and I lived in the Himalayas with my master. Is this my true nature? I have a body and a particular face. I am called Swami Rama. But this is not my true nature. When I was born, I was so little; that changed. I used to go to school; that changed. I became an adult; that changed. I became old; that is still changing. This cannot be my essential nature.

Essential nature means "that which is not subject to death, change, and decay, that which cannot be changed in any condition, that which is everlasting." Your essential nature is beyond your body, breath, senses, and mind. When you know that you are not your body, that your body is something different from you, and that your breath, senses, and mind are different from you, then you will be a seer. Such a seer, who has learned not to identify with the body, breath, senses, and mind is established in his essential nature, which is peace, happiness, and bliss.

Patanjali says it is your mind, what he calls chitta and its modifications, that stands between you and Reality. Mind and its modifications should be controlled because without control you identify yourself with the objects of the world. You do not identify with your true Self. Once you have nirodhah, once you have learned how to control that wandering mind and how to direct it consciously, then what happens? When you understand your mind and its various functions and modifications, you come to know the two powers of your mind. One power makes you negative and creates obstacles for you; the other power helps you in removing those obstacles. You have all the potentials at your disposal. Learn to concentrate your mind. Mind is a very powerful instrument. If you are the owner of your mind, you should know how to use it. If mind owns the body, then you belong to mind. Study the power of your senses; study the power of your mind. When mind is controlled, it does not create any obstacles. If mind does not create any obstacle, the center of consciousness will come forward and reveal itself to you. When mind is led toward awareness of the center of consciousness, mind can fathom many, many levels. Today you function on a sense level where pain is not bearable; if you go to another dimension, you will see that pain changes. A level of consciousness comes in which pain becomes relative. There is another level of consciousness where you see things as they are, not as you want to see them. You may think that one person is good and another person is bad. This is your way of seeing. You do not see that every human being is exclusive and cannot be compared; everybody is beautiful. When you open the real eye within, you will see things as they are. Everything is beautiful; there is nothing ugly. Ugliness is in your eyes because of a particular thought or desire. You see things as you want to see them, not as they are. Another level of consciousness comes in which there is clarity of mind and you see things as they are; there is no longer any confusion. You see two individuals, but you perceive the unity beneath the two. You can never hate anyone if you are aware of one universal consciousness. Still another level of consciousness comes in which you are one with Reality all the time; you are liberated. To reach this level of consciousness first you need to be free from all fears, and second, you need to liberate yourself from the concept that you are separate from the whole. In this way you will fathom one level of consciousness, then another, and then you will become part of eternity.

Study the power of the deeper levels of your consciousness and you will come to know that the source from which consciousness flows in various degrees is the most powerful. That source is one and the same as the cosmic source. We are all ripples in the vast ocean of bliss called Brahman, the summum bonum of life, the very source of all life force, from where all ripples rise, play, and again subside. Learn to identify with the source of light and life.

Life is like a wheel. In the center of the wheel there is a hub that does not move, but wherever you go that center is with you. The center itself never moves, but it moves when the wheel rotates. It goes with the wheel. How will you classify and define that center which moves, yet does not move? It is the cause of all movements but it does not move itself. You cannot study that thing which moves. That which moves is not everlasting, is not Truth. Body, senses, and mind move. They are not the everlasting part of the Self. That which does not move is immortal. Deep within us, that which is the center of consciousness, does not move. It is not subject to change or decay; it does not go to destruction. Your essential nature is the center of consciousness within. You have consciousness now, but that consciousness is so low that you are not aware of your true nature. You are only aware of the body. You cannot say that you have no awareness. You all have awareness of your individuality. That is why you project yourself. That is why you say, *This is me, this is not me.* You are aware. Just by saying that you are aware you do not receive anything. How much are you aware? Are you aware of all the levels of your being? Are you aware of that center from which consciousness flows in various degrees and grades? That is perfect awareness. Until you have realized that center, you are not spiritually aware. You are not enlightened. You have to know yourself on all levels in this lifetime and get enlightened here and now. You should have that determination.

You cannot understand your whole being on all levels; you cannot reach the fountainhead of life and light, the center of consciousness within, without knowing that the world around you is not real. That which looks real is not real. It can never be Truth. *Absolute Truth* means "that which is not subject to change, that which is self-existent, that which was never born and so never dies." A human being is a perfect, yet unfinished being. A human being has all the capacity to attain wisdom, to reach the fountainhead of light and life that gives freedom from all fears, pains, and miseries. You depend too much on gods — not God, but gods. God is within you. You are human and at the same time you are God because God is within you. A human being has three natures — animal, human and divine. From this viewpoint a human being is complete. If he identifies with the animal nature, then he behaves like an animal. If he identifies with the human nature, then he becomes human. If he becomes aware of godly powers, then he becomes divine. You are searching for something without understanding that it is within you. Search within. This is a direct approach. Do not search for God outside. God is already within you. When you come to know that God dwells within you, then your life will totally change and you will be transformed. You will not feel your individual existence but you will feel that God exists in you. You are a living shrine. God walks with you and witnesses all your actions. All the great religions say the same thing. They repeat the same story again and again — that a human being is the finest creature of God. All the scriptures say that God is omnipresent, omniscient, and omnipotent. God is everywhere. Then where are you? Where is the place for you to exist? How can you claim that you or I exist somewhere and this is yours and that is mine? The moment you realize that you don't exist, but God exists, you will be free. You all have some awareness. You all have those potentials. You all have the means to realize the Self. You have to realize the great glory that is hidden deep within. It is the mind that is creating the barriers.

Patanjali says to come home and realize that you can establish yourself in your essential nature by having control over your mind and modifications. The central theme of the *Yoga Sutras* is to learn to control your mind and modifications. When you have perfect control over the modifications of the mind, you will attain the highest level of consciousness or samadhi. If you have control over your mind and its modifications, you will establish yourself in your essential nature, which is full of peace, happiness, and bliss. When you establish yourself in your essential nature you will gain freedom from all miseries and you will be fit to attain a state of samadhi. You will attain happiness, you will attain samadhi, you will attain enlightenment.

You wonder how you will do it and what you must do to attain samadhi. You say it is not possible for you to attain samadhi and you give up. You think it is not possible for you to become a yogi because you think you have to renounce the world. Patanjali has never said that. Whatever path you follow—the path of bhakti, the path of prayer, the path of good conduct of life in the external world—you will first have to learn something about mind and its modifications.

Without controlling your mind and modifications, both conscious and unconscious, you cannot attain samadhi. You say it is not possible for you to have control over your unconscious mind. You have to learn how to use your conscious mind properly, not by philosophizing, but by simply training the conscious mind. First you will have to understand the method of controlling the turmoil that is tormenting your conscious mind. Otherwise you cannot know what is hidden, what is in the unconscious, the unknown part of your mind. The moment you become aware that this is your mind, that these are the qualities of mind, that the mind functions like this, and you understand the difference between the conscious and unconscious mind, it becomes possible for you to understand and to control the unconscious mind.

Don't say that it is too difficult. Don't say that it is useless. Don't say that you cannot do it. Don't postpone it for the next life. Don't say that millions of people cannot control their mind, so I also cannot. Don't say that! You are able to do it. Don't give up and say that mind cannot be controlled. Mind can be controlled. You can become master over your mind and learn how to use your mind and its modifications to attain the highest state of samadhi. Even the best of your actions in the world are in vain if your mind is not at peace. Patanjali gives you a definite method of attaining the highest state. To be successful in both the external world and the internal world, you have to understand mind and its modifications and have control. By having conscious control over mind and its modifications you can attain a state called samadhi, which is free from all conflicts within and without. Once you have control you will know your essential nature. Those who have known their essential nature are attained sages. Those who do not know suffer on account of ignorance. They are in darkness, but darkness is actually the absence of light. When you are not aware of the Reality, you create darkness for yourself.

You are Identifying Yourself with the
OBJECTS OF THE WORLD,
Forgetting Your True Nature

The fourth sutra says, *vritti-sarupyam itaratra*. You are constantly identifying yourself with the objects of the world; that is why you are suffering. You are miserable and ignorant because you constantly identify yourself with the objects of the world and with your thought forms. You identify yourself with the objects of the world and forget your true nature because you have no control over your mind and its modifications. When you forget your true nature and identify yourself with the objects of the world, then you are confused. In this state of confusion you feel sad, bewildered, and lost. Why should you not identify with the objects of the world? If you identify yourself with the blackboard, what will happen to you? You will become lifeless and inert. Identifying yourself with objects will always bring pain.

You know yourself through your body. You constantly identify yourself with your body. You are *not* body. You have a body, but you are not the body. You use all your resources to look after this body from morning to evening. No matter how much you look after this body, the result will be death. Don't look after this body because you are attached to it; look after your body because it is an instrument. Body is your instrument, but you are not the body.

The ultimate cause of misery is that you identify yourself with the objects of the world and with your thought patterns, forgetting your true nature. A thought wave comes from the past and you identify yourself with it. *How miserable I was in 1965 when I was in India. How miserable I was when I was there.* Why are you being miserable now? If you think of the devil all the time, create an image and fantasize and strengthen that image, you will identify with the devil. You create certain images in your mind in your daily life. *I am weak. I am weak. I am weak.* This biofeedback is going on constantly and you move toward degeneration. You become nothing but the way you think, feel, and understand. You are identifying yourself with your thoughts. You keep giving yourself these suggestions. *I am bad. I am good for nothing. I am ugly. Nobody likes me. Everyone hates me.* If nobody likes you, it does not mean that everyone hates you. *No. Everyone hates me. Everyone is looking at me. Everyone is picking on me.* You are constantly identifying yourself with your thought patterns. *I am good. I am bad. I am ugly. I am beautiful.* You have forgotten your true nature. You are constantly being tossed by your thought patterns. This goes on and on and becomes a sickness.

To examine the power of suggestion, my master once did an experiment with me.

My master told one of the swamis, "Tell him he is a bad boy, and let me see how he reacts."

An old swami would come and say to me, "You are a bad boy," and I would feel bad even though I had not done anything bad! I was mischievous all right but I had not done anything. I said, "Swamiji, I did not do anything. I respect you. I respect everybody. I work hard for you people. Why are you telling me I am bad?"

Another swami said, "Do not listen to him; you are a good boy."

I went to my master and said, "For no reason one swami is telling me I am a bad boy, and another swami is telling me I am a good boy."

He said, "You are a fool! I told them to give you these two suggestions. First, you accepted that you are bad, and when another person said that you are good, you also accepted that. You are neither good nor bad. You are stupid. You are a fool!"

I said, "What shall I do?"

He said, "Don't accept any suggestions from others. Learn to judge yourself whether you are good or bad. By your bad actions, which are not to be done, you are bad. By your good actions, you are good already."

Look at how much you lean on the suggestions of others. If somebody says, "You are bad," you are horrified! If somebody says, "You are very good," how much joy you feel! Everyone wants to be praised. Even swamis are affected.

If you think and live the way people want you to, you cannot live in this world. You cannot survive! Don't worry about opposition. The more you find opposition, the more your path is clear. Don't be reactionary. Learn to build your own opinion about yourself and watch your progress. You have to be strong. You cannot survive if you accept suggestions from the world. You have to watch how others express their opinion about you and how you express your opinion about yourself. Exaggerated suggestions blast your mind, and mind is weak. It has not been trained in accepting gifts. It is a gift if somebody says you are good or bad. Whether somebody gives you a good gift or a bad gift, you will have to learn to filter that. Why do you want to make your mind a garbage disposal center by accepting whatever others say?

Buddha, the Enlightened One, was the only son of his father who was a ruler. He was born into a royal family. He renounced everything and started to beg. He started begging to kill his ego, to tame his ego, to purify his ego. It is very difficult. If I tell you to beg, you cannot do that. Ananda, the first disciple of Buddha, and the Buddha went with their begging bowls in their hands at Rajgiri, Bihar. "Biksham, biksham dehi." It is a custom that if somebody comes to your door, you have to give them something. Once when he went to a door to beg alms, the lady of the house said, "I am fed up with all these beggars. The whole city is full of beggars."

This woman was tired. She became angry and said, "Whatever I have cooked for my family and for myself, all these mundis have taken away. I have nothing to give. I am sick of these people!"

Everybody wanted to follow Buddha and to imitate him, so the city was full of beggars. She had nothing left to give because she had already given everything that she had. Her child was passing his stool, so she picked up some feces with a spoon and said, "Here, Buddha, you deserve this. Come on. Take it. I have nothing else to give."

Ananda lost his temper and said, "You woman, you are behaving like that to my Lord, the Enlightened One? You have insulted my Lord. I am going to curse you. You will go to hell!"

Buddha looked calmly toward her. "Do not talk like that. If she is giving me something, it depends on me whether I take it or not." He gently said, "Ma, mother, please keep it for yourself. I do not need it."

Buddha looked at Ananda and said, "Ananda, why did you call her a bad woman and curse her that she will go to hell? One who can lose his temper like this has no power to curse. That shows your ego. You are not my disciple. If somebody wants to give you something and if you do not want to take it, just ignore him. Why are you worried? When somebody speaks harshly to you, why do you lose your temper? Because you are weak, so you accept it. Don't do that. Learn not to be disturbed by anybody. One who disturbs you is stronger than you. Don't bow before anybody's negative strength."

He said, "Master, you are my Lord. I cannot bear such insult."

"I was not insulted. If somebody wants to give you something unpleasant, please do not take it."

You should have that attitude in your daily life. If somebody says something pleasant, accept it. If someone says something unpleasant, instead of getting upset, reject it. Do not allow yourself to be affected by it. Observe yourself: if somebody says you are stupid, you feel sad. How weak you are! If everyone says you are a great man, you become egotistical. That greatness has been thrust upon you by suggestions; it is not sound. Do not live your life on suggestions. If someone says you are good, then you smile. If they say you are bad, then you feel sad. You think others should admire you, but that is a weakness. You should learn to admire yourself by becoming aware of the best part of yourself. Why should you depend on others all the time? If they don't admire you, what will happen to you? Such admiration is only superficial.

Many of you do not have any opinion about yourself at all, because you have always lived on the opinion of others. What others think of you, that is what you think you are. You have never learned the process of forming your own opinion. Patanjali says those fake crutches are very unhealthy because in the end, during the period of transition, you need your own opinion. You need to understand how to form your own opinions, how to express your own opinions, and how to execute your own opinions. Don't be tossed by the opinions of others. Learn to understand the Reality within and see that Reality outside. It is possible with simple awareness.

You are not aware of your essential nature. The difference between you and a yogi is this: A yogi is aware of the Reality. You are not aware of the Reality because you identify yourself with the objects of your mind. Lack of awareness and knowledge is the cause of your suffering. That is called ignorance. Ignorance is self-created, is self-delusion. You have not become *drashta,* a seer. You can become drishta if you stop identifying yourself with the objects of the world. By not identifying with the objects of the world, you can establish yourself in your true nature.

If you have control over the modifications of the mind, you can attain a state of samadhi and establish yourself in your essential nature. You can attain a state of samadhi that is free from all conflicts and problems. If you do not do it, what will happen to you? If you are not in samadhi, then you constantly identify yourself with the physical world and its objects, which are not everlasting, which are not permanent, which are subject to death, change, and decay. It means you are not aware of that which is eternal, unchanging, and everlasting. The objects of the world have no power to control your life, but you get attached to the world. You identify yourself with the objects of the world and you become a victim. Once you get attached you create a whirlpool around yourself and you are miserable.

My master was from Bengal. He was a judge whose only son was hanged at Darjeeling for shooting the governor. He broke his pen, left, and went to the Himalayas where he meditated for many, many years.

Then he met my biological father. When my mother was forty-eight, he blessed my father and mother, and I was born. When I became an orphan, he brought me up. I feel blessed. I never remember my parents. I never missed my mother or father because whenever I think of father, my master's image comes to me. He played all the roles for me. I never feel lonely.

One day I was standing with my master at the foot of the Dronagiri Mountain, which was very hard to climb. I said, "Let me climb this."

He said, "Can you climb it?"

I said, "Of course!" So I climbed the mountain and I stayed on the peak.

He said, "Who is with you there?"

I said, "I am all alone."

He said, "Are you lonely?"

I said, "Yes."

He said, "No. You are alone, but you are not lonely."

When you learn to be alone, but all in one, then you will not be lonely. Who makes you lonely? Not strangers. The person whom you love or who loves you makes you lonely. It means your attitude toward your relationships is not right. Something is wrong somewhere. The object of love is supposed to help you, but instead that object constantly makes you lonely. If your husband doesn't come home on time and doesn't pay attention toward you, what will happen? You will become lonely. Neighbors do not make you lonely. Your own people who claim to love you make you lonely. You will remain lonely as long as you depend on external crutches. You are always lonely even if you are with many people. You try not to be lonely by getting married and establishing a home. You have all the means, yet you are lonely. The greatest of all diseases is loneliness. Why are you lonely? Once you know the center within you, you will never remain lonely. If you know the friend within, you will never be lonely. You are lonely when you isolate yourself from the whole by constantly identifying yourself with the objects of your mind and the objects of the world. I will give you an example.

Someone went to a swami and said, "Sir, I have been dying to learn the method of meditation."

Swami said, "Go to a small room — not a big room. Don't hang any pictures in the room. Sit down there and meditate on a bull for seven days. Then you will learn the effects of meditation."

"Only the effects?"

He said, "No. You will realize what meditation is. First you will know, then I will give you the right method."

The man went there and after six days of intense meditation he said, "I cannot come out. My horns are too big. My body is huge."

He had assumed the form of a bull by meditating on a bull.

At present you are doing the same thing. You have assumed certain forms. *I am weak. I am weak. I am weak.* You keep repeating this throughout the whole day. *I can't do this. Honey, I am suffering. Please help.* You lean on others. You are suffering because you are not tapping the resources within yourself.

In this system, Patanjali wants to show you Reality. He says, "The seen is for your sake, oh seer!" This is all the seen. This is all for your sake. You are not for the sake of the seen. You become a victim of the superficiality of the things of the world. You are living in the world and you forget the Reality. That is why you cannot enjoy the things of the world. This world of enjoyment is for your sake, but what happens? You identify yourself with the objects of the world that are meant to be instruments. You forget that you are a seer. Objects are definitely different from the seer. You identify with the world that is quickly changing and then you forget your real Self. When the seer starts to understand his own essential nature, then he becomes free from identifying with the objects of the world.

You think that you cannot attain the highest state of tranquility, though you have all the capacity and potential within. To decide is a one-second's job. It is not difficult. There is no need to make your life topsy-turvy or renounce your home. Just be aware of the Reality. You can do that. When you learn to establish yourself in your essential nature you will get freedom from all miseries and you will be fit enough to attain a state of samadhi.

Patanjali says not to identify with the objects of the world; they are fleeting and subject to change, death, and decay. Don't identify with something that is changing. Identify with your true nature that is Truth, and that is not subject to change or death. In actuality you are Atman, a child of eternity. To remember, to be aware of the center, is the only way of freedom. When awareness is turned inward, that is called freedom.

These four sutras are the foundation of Patanjali's philosophy. If you understand these four sutras, you will understand the entire book in principle, but to practice, you will still have to learn more.

Practice Means to Awaken
the CONSCIENCE

You will have to practice for a long time. *Abhyasa-vairagyabhyam tan nirodhah*. Practice means repetition of the same thing again and again and again to form a strong habit. Habits are motivation in life. If you do not have determination to attain that which should be attained, if you are not constantly aware of the Reality, how can you practice? You will feel lazy and you will not be able to sit in meditation.

There is one alarm in your system, something coming from within that guides all the time. There is one teacher within that you call your conscience. Whenever you want to do something that should not be done, immediately from inside something says, *Don't do that*. It silently says *no*. It is not a part of mind. Rather it is your conscience that is telling your mind, whispering to your mind. You have been avoiding that. Habit patterns are so strong that the voice of silence, the voice of the conscience, is not heard. You do not need anyone from outside to tell you what not to do. You know that you should not lie; yet you lie. Once mind listens to these secret whispers, then you are introduced to the real teacher within, your own conscience. All teachings are meant for that day when you start listening to your conscience. It does not mean that you should not listen to the external teacher who is teaching you. Your teacher is trying to make you aware that there is something within you, a teacher within, who is a great friend. No matter who you are, your conscience is always there. If you learn to listen to the voice of the conscience, you can transform your whole personality. That conscience knows everything. No book can teach you; no teacher can teach you. Conscience knows and knows that it knows. Even when you go to a teacher to ask something, you draw your own conclusions and follow your conscience.

But you do not always listen to the teachings of your conscience. In fact, you are constantly killing your conscience. According to the great books of wisdom, the greatest sin of all is to kill your conscience. After some time your conscience stops talking to you because you do not listen to it. You have ignored your conscience so much that it has become silent. It continues to witness your actions but does not say anything. Learn to listen to your conscience. Most of the time you are confused by your mind. Sometimes your mind plays tricks on you and pretends to be your conscience. Mind says, *I can steal some of his money. Nobody is watching me. Why does he need to have millions of dollars? If I steal only one hundred thousand dollars, so what?*

Mind is different from conscience. Your conscience always wants to help you to improve yourself and unfold your inner being. Mind always tries to persuade you not to practice. You know that it is not good for you to avoid your practice, and yet the mind says, *Come on. Postpone it until tomorrow.* Postponement is the nature of the mind. Some students do their practice for some time and then they leave it. After some time, they start doing it again. Then they say, "Okay. Let us vacation for some time, honey. Let us not do any practice." Again they start practicing. I call those who postpone enlightenment indefinitely fourth-class students.

Mind always leads you toward your habits, your senses, and sense objects. Perhaps you like to eat fish, but the doctor has said not to take it. The doctor's advice has been heard by your conscience. Your mind does not want to hear it and does not care for doctors. *There are many doctors. Why should I listen to them? Let me have some fish today. Nothing is going to happen to me.* Your conscience speaks to you all the time. Conscience is like a mirror that shows you your face exactly as it is. When you look at yourself in the mirror, the mirror does not create anything for you. It is like a thermometer that registers heat and cold. It tells you who you are, what you are, and what you should be. Whenever you want to do something, your conscience says, *Do not do this. It is not good.* But your mind says, *No. Let me do it.*

Conscience cannot be false. It never misguides from the very beginning. Even a bad man who is considered to be the worst person in society is not misguided by his conscience. But you fail to listen to your conscience, and ignore your conscience because of bad habits. When your conscience becomes dim, your reason does not function properly and it misguides you. When reason misguides, the mind cannot function and becomes crazy. All your actions and speech are disoriented and you cannot function properly. Perhaps you are doing something and suddenly a distressing thought intrudes. You are temporarily distracted and then you come back. Then, another thought comes and you go another way. You misuse the time and opportunity you have of being a human being. You have all the potentials and all the means but you misuse them. I always ask my students to listen to their conscience when they feel weak in the beginning. The first few days they start to condemn themselves. I say, "This is not the way. There is a wonderful part of you; there is something beautiful in you; there is something very special in you. Why do you not try to see that thing?" Practice means to awaken the conscience, to allow the conscience to speak to you. When your conscience awakens it says, *Look, do not repeat that again and again and again.* By repetition you have formed a strong habit. Your conscience and that habit fight constantly. Your habit wins and conscience loses. After some time, conscience stops talking to you. Conscience tells you things all the time and conscience knows, but you do not know your conscience. The voice of your mind is very loud. The voice of the conscience comes from silence. The first step of enlightenment is to follow the conscience and not the mind. At the highest level of consciousness, conscience becomes brilliant.

Anybody who has started listening to the conscience is very close to the Reality. Your conscience is within you. It is not an external friend. All your external friends amuse you. A friend within is real company. You say, "Two's company and three's a crowd." When you and your conscience are there, there are two and they are real company. When the mind, the third, comes, then it becomes a crowd.

When you start practicing you will stumble many times. I have stumbled many times, even despite having a great force behind me—my master, several other sages, and the grace of God. I had a fire within so that no matter how many times I stumbled I would get up again. I did not give up. You give up too soon.

You close your eyes and if you do not see anything in meditation, you say, *My method is not good. My mantra is not good.* You go on collecting mantras. You do not do meditation but you have a long collection of mantras. You have wasted so much money, and you have not done any real meditation. In abhyasa and meditation, on this path of enlightenment, you have to be very patient and strong and persistent. When a child stumbles, she gets up again because she wants to walk. It is her right to walk. It is your right to walk on the path and finally reach the goal. Do not postpone it for the next lifetime. Do it here and now, in this lifetime. You do not attain anything overnight; you will stumble many times like a child stumbles when she starts learning to walk. When you practice you will experience, and when you experience you will find that conscience is strengthened and guides you again and again.

Out of curiosity you always want to learn something new. When you learn something that you did not know you say, "This is a wonderful thing that I have learned." You do not want to practice what you already know. The truth is you will not acquire any knowledge in your life that you have not already acquired in your childhood. You already have the basic principles, the guidelines, and the foundation of your knowledge, but you do not practice. To practice it is not necessary to create a rigid discipline. You should just observe and understand how to use the knowledge that you have.

Gradually you can practice. Technique alone does not help. The basic principles needed are sincerity, faithfulness, truthfulness, and punctuality. Even if you know the technique of throwing something at the target, if you do not practice, it will hit somewhere else. Practice is necessary and practice makes perfect. Slowly increase your limit. Do not force yourself to sit for two hours one day, and then do no practice at all for a week. That should not be the way. It is said that a first-class student can attain this state of mind in three months' time, while conducting all his duties, a second-class student in six months, and a third-class student in three years. A fourth-class student can never attain. If you regularly practice and watch your practice and the condition of your mind, you can do it. The question is how much importance you give to your practice. How much anxiety do you have for your practice or for other things? What is important in your life? Do you really want to transform your personality and improve yourself, or do you only want to improve your conditions? If you do not improve yourself, your conditions and your environment will never be improved. It is better to improve yourself so that your conditions and environment do not become malignant to you. To improve your conditions, first learn to understand your essential nature by understanding the various levels of your being and by developing control over mind and its modifications.

There are various paths to the same mountaintop, but there is only one realization. There are various ways and methods to attain that. The path of action or the path of the world is as perfect as the path of renunciation. In the path of action you learn not to be attached and perform your duties. In the path of renunciation you learn to renounce all that you think is yours and to devote all your time and energy toward Self-realization with a one-pointed mind. It is a very difficult path. It is rare to be a renunciate. Only a fortunate few can truly walk on the razor's edge of the path of renunciation. It is a very sharp and very narrow path. It is easier and more common to be in the world, to live in the world, and yet remain above. There is no difference at all. Do not condemn yourself because you are in the world, or think that you cannot do anything. Learn to discipline yourself; learn to organize yourself; learn to understand your resources; learn to know your inner potentials; and learn to make a schedule for life. *This is my aim and I have to attain this. All my resources should be applied for attaining the aim of life.*

The way of adjustment leads you to contentment. The way of adjustment is the way of the world — the way of action, the way of karma. You learn how to function in the external world. You understand that you are a citizen of two worlds — the world within yourself and the world outside, and you learn to create a bridge between these two worlds. You have not to be lost in the world, yet you have to unfold yourself to that extent where you can realize your real Self. You no longer identify with the objects of the world or with your mind. You learn to understand life as it is with all its currents and cross currents. You understand how to live in the external world and how to compose yourself so that you remain with your center all the time.

Most people follow the path of action. They live in the world, which is full of charms, temptations, and attractions, and they are constantly blasted by the opinions of others. Someone says you are good and someone else says you are bad. There are two extremes. To constantly be tossed by the suggestions of the world so that you spend all your time executing the opinions of others is dangerous. Likewise, you can isolate yourself and say, *Now I don't want to listen to the world because my whole life I have listened to the world. I am not going to listen anymore.* This might lead toward egocentricity or cripple your process of growth. You have to evaluate the opinions of all if you live in the world. Are you being selfish when you are not listening to others? Is the other person selfish? If he is not selfish, listen to him. If someone is selfless and loves you and says, "These days you seem to be isolating yourself," listen to that person. If you say you don't want to listen to anybody, it is not possible. How can you live in this world? You can do it not through the help of samnyasa, but with the help of *vairagya*.

The Pull of the Strings of
ATTACHMENT is Very Strong

Two things are practiced on both paths—meditation and the philosophy of vairagya or nonattachment. Whether you are on the path of renunciation or the path of action, in order to practice truth, to know the mysteries of life, to attain the goal of life, you have to learn vairagya. Patanjali says, *abhyasa-vairagya.* If the philosophy of nonattachment is accurately practiced, you can be free from the influences of all the vrittis and you can attain samadhi.

Vairagya does not make you a swami nor does it lead you toward the philosophy of renunciation. It leads you to the philosophy of action—how to function in the world yet remain unaffected. I will explain the difference between samnyasa (renunciation) and vairagya (nonattachment). I have renounced my home because I want to be a swami, but I still remember it. It is always in my mind. The home is still there and I am here. What have I done? I simply created a space. This is samnyasa, or mere renunciation. In vairagya, you live in a home wherever you are and yet you remain above. Therefore, vairagya is definitely higher than samnyasa. It is good to have samnyasa, but without vairagya it is of no use for you to renounce. If a swami who has renounced the world does not know the philosophy of nonattachment and simply renounces, he will not be successful.

In the path of renunciation you renounce all the objects and all your relationships — your property, your relatives, and your relationships with people. It is very difficult. It is easy to renounce your home and then think of your home all the time. That is not renunciation but the height of emotions. You renounce your home and then you think, *What a wonderful home I have renounced.* Attachment is very powerful. It tempts and charms the sadhaka all the time. The pull of the strings of attachment is very, very strong. When Buddha decided to renounce his home he got up at night to walk out. His wife and child were both in deep sleep. He turned back from the door to see the face of his son for the last time. The call of attachment pulled him back because the strings of attachment are very strong. Others were surprised. This man had decided to renounce, yet he had a lust to see his son's face again. It took him a long time to decide.

In the path of action you learn to perform the duty that you have assumed for yourself. That which you have not assumed for yourself is not your duty. Before you were born, before you came to this world, you chose to come to a certain family in a certain society. Go according to the duties that are corresponding. Do your duties and help others. If you are married, be nice to the person with whom you are married. Be sincere and look after your children. If you are not married, study and try to grow and understand the values of life. Know what your duties are and how to perform them. But even if you know your duties, your habits are so bad they do not allow you to perform your duties properly. Whatever you do you should do it under control. Control does not mean that you should not do your duties. If your business is to sell meat and to cut chicken into pieces everyday, that is your duty. Examine yourself, your circumstances, and your inner being, and then do it. Your conscience will tell you what you are doing. Your conscience tells you everything.

Your personality has been woven by your habit patterns and you have become a victim of your habits. How can you help yourself? Follow the philosophy of vairagya by practicing it. It is not possible for anyone to live happily under the pressures of fears, stresses, and strains. That is not considered to be living. If you practice the philosophy of nonattachment, you will live happily. Start your practice from the people with whom you live and whom you love. Your home should be a nucleus, emanating love to each other. Have two sets of rules for yourself — one for home that you use with your people, and another for outside in the world. At home you do not have to protect yourself or feel insecure. Take action first. Give without thinking and do not suspect anything. When you are moving outside, suspect first, think twice, take action last. Look at the difference.

Vairagya means you are doing your duties yet you are not attached to the things therein. It is not necessary for you to renounce. Patanjali's teachings are meant for those who live in the world. He was very cautious not to use the word *samnyasa*. No human being can live without doing actions and he has to reap the fruits of the actions. Is there any religion that says that you should not do your duty? All the great cultures and religions of the world say, "As you sow, so shall you reap." It is a law accepted by all religions. You cannot live without doing anything. Everyone is bound to do some action. From morning until evening you are doing something and reaping the fruits. You are not free. Even if you are sleeping, you are doing some action. Sleep is also an action. Even one who is a renunciate has to do something. He renounces only name and fame and property — all that is directly related to him. He does not renounce teaching others, or being gentle, or learning to help others.

When you do your duty you become victim of your duty. A woman says, "I have to go home, Swamiji. My husband will be at home. My children will be at home now. My house has been ignored."

I say, "Oh, please sit down."

"No, no, Swamiji. I will see you later on. I respect you, but you know, I have to do this."

This "have to do" makes you a slave. You cannot live without doing your duty, yet duty makes you a slave. Are you not fed up of leading this sort of dull life, repeating the same thing everyday? You are. But what can you do? Who creates duty for you? You do. You create bondage for yourself. You don't want that bondage, yet you are doing it and you call it duty. But there is a way that is called freedom. In your practical life you are told to do your duty and yet be free. How can you be free? If you go on doing your duty and all the actions that you do, you are bound to reap the fruits from them. To be free, those fruits should be offered to those whom you love. Charity begins from home.

Here is another point: you feel it is boring to do your duty. You are doing your duty and the fruits come. You give them to your children and husband, but you do not feel joy. You feel like you are a slave and you are being used by these people. What is the way? You will have to learn to grease your duty with love. Any duty you are doing without love creates a very serious problem. Human beings are contracting and going away from the law of expansion that is called love. *Possession* means "contraction;" *love* means "expansion." If you really want to learn to live, learn to do your duties lovingly. Create love for your duties, whatever you do, and then they will not give you tension or bring stress to your life.

You create stress for yourself because you do not know how to perform your duties, though you have imposed them on yourself. The only way is to learn to love your duties. If you only love the objects of joy, and you think that your partner is an object like your home, your furniture, and other things in life, you can never be happy. Human beings are not objects. Human beings are higher than objects. Learn to love those persons for whom you perform your duties and take all the objects of the world as means. Never be attached to the means, for means are only means. You love the means because they help you. But if the same means become obstacles for you, they are no longer helpful. In the path of the world, the path of enlightenment through action, learn how to perform your duties with love and without being attached to the objects of the world. The objects of the world are only means. They do not belong to you. They are only for you to use. Learn to enjoy them as means and do not get attached to them or claim ownership on them. This sense of 'mine' and 'thine' creates serious problems for you. When you do your duties with love there will be no stress and you will be free.

So my first point is, you cannot stop doing your actions. Secondly, all the fruits of your actions should be given to others. Thirdly, learn to grease your duty with love. There is a formula. Skillful action done selflessly becomes a means, a sort of worship. Those who do skillful action selflessly and lovingly are free from the bondage of karma.

When you do your actions, perform them as a duty, lovingly, skillfully, and without any attachment. You can learn to live peacefully in this world, attaining your goal of life in this lifetime, in a few years' time, in a few months' time, in a few days' time, even in a second's time, if you understand the philosophy of vairagya or nonattachment. To be nonattached you do not have to leave the world or impose many "don'ts." You do not have to follow any rigid discipline. Discipline should not be rigid or create tension or stress. Disciplining yourself means guiding all the powers and resources that you have toward your goal. Discipline is something unique that helps you to keep your powers from being dissipated. You should understand discipline before you follow it. Do not make too many big rules for yourself. That will only weaken your willpower. Do not decide that you are going to do something and then not complete the task. Once you decide to do something you have to do it. No one should stop you. You are killing your conscience and your willpower all the time by deciding, *I am going to do this, I am going to do this, I am going to do this,* but never accomplishing anything. Every day you make a resolution and you never accomplish anything because you do not strengthen your will, you do not have determination, you do not coordinate and apply all the resources you have. You do not work with mind, action, and speech together. That is the reason for your failure.

If you really want to live happily in the world, you have to practice vairagya. Gathering the twigs of success in the external world and having all the worldly means of comfort can become a problem for one who does not know the philosophy of nonattachment. St. Bernard said, "Learn to use the things of the world, but love God alone." He understood the philosophy of nonattachment. You mistakenly take this to mean that the whole world is meant for you to use. With this idea you cheat others and think that you are successful. If you think that the whole world is meant for you to use, why do you not think that you are also meant to be used by the world? You should compromise. Neither should you use the world nor should you allow anyone to use you. It is very important to learn the philosophy of nonattachment.

You are committing two mistakes — possessing something that does not belong to you, and being attached to that; or even just using it and being attached. When something is not yours, what right do you have to be attached to it? This unauthorized possession makes you small. There is one thing that you should remember. *I am so grateful to You, oh Lord, for all the things of the world. You have given me the best of things. I have the right to use them and I should make them a means, but I have no right to possess them because they are not mine. I cannot create even a blade of grass. How can I say anything is mine? All the things of the world are meant for me, and I can use them as means, but I will not possess them nor will I be attached.*

Why do you create attachments? If you do not have a child of your own, you are not satisfied. You do not think, *God has given me this opportunity. Since I do not have a child I will devote my time to the Lord.* Instead, you want to adopt somebody else's child and create more attachment for yourself. You want to possess something. If you see something pleasing in your neighbor's house, you want to have it. You do not realize that these superficial things will create more attachment and dissipate the energy of your mind.

Life means relationships. It is like a coin with two sides. Even a swami who has renounced the world and has nothing to do with home, wife, children, honors, or name and fame, still has relationships. His body is related to his mind and his body, breath, and senses are related to his mind and soul. How can he say he can live without relationships?

Many of you think if you practice nonattachment, you will not be able to love your husband or wife. Vairagya does not mean that you cannot love your husband or wife. You love them more because you understand your relationship better. When you understand that something is weak, at least you will not lean heavily on it. If you see that something is strong, you can lean with full confidence. If you do not know whether it is strong or weak, you might lean heavily and fall down and break it. That is what happens in your relationships. That which you call love is lust, not love. Attachment brings misery; nonattachment means love. Love has two characteristics—giving and freedom. Love teaches you how to give without any reservations. Love does not bind you. Love does not victimize anyone. Love gives you freedom and makes you selfless. If love does not give you freedom, that is not love. Love makes you aware of the Reality, the Truth. Learn to love yet remain unattached.

Nonattachment, the philosophy of love, is one of the greatest philosophies of Christianity. Christ said,

"Don't get attached to the body. Love the soul alone." Through love you can reach God, but not through love of objects. There are two types of love—love with object and love without object. Do you need an object to love? A husband needs his wife's body to love her. A wife needs her husband's body to love him. A child needs his father's body to love him. This is called love with object. But all objects change; all objects go through death, decay, and decomposition. You married somebody who looked very beautiful. Suddenly she got smallpox and now she looks ugly. You leave her for another girl. Did you love the previous person? No, it was actually your lust that motivated you to get married, but you called it love.

Indifference is not the same thing as nonattachment. Indifference is carelessness. Nonattachment is knowledge; nonattachment means love. When you are fed up with someone, you become indifferent. You have not been able to find a way out of the situation so you become indifferent. When a woman becomes indifferent to her husband whom she wants to leave, he knows it. He can feel that she is different. She doesn't smile. She doesn't move properly. She doesn't listen to him. Indifference comes from carelessness. Nonattachment means you love all the things around you because they have been given to you by God, but you know they are not yours. They belong to God. You enjoy all the things given to you by God with great love. In attachment you think: *These things are mine; I own them. I should use them.* You have no knowledge of who has given them to you.

If all things change and are quickly fleeing, how can you live in the world? First, you should know that you have come to play a particular role in the world. If you are a woman, you cannot play a man's role. You may be able to play it efficiently, but perhaps it is not good for you. You are assuming a relationship that is not good. Likewise, if a man is playing a woman's role, it is not considered to be good because he is not efficient in playing that role. If we all learn to play our roles nicely, perhaps the world will be transformed into a Garden of Eden. This can take place with the philosophy of nonattachment, which is called true love. To love others you will have to first learn to love yourself. If you do not love yourself, you cannot love your partner or anybody else. Gandhi said, "I always say I love myself. Not that I am a particular being, but that God is in me."

You are a mobile shrine. Infinity lives in this mobile shrine. Is it not a wonder, the greatest of all miracles, that Immortality, Infinity, dwells within the mortal frame, the finite body? Infinity dwells within the finite. Wherever the finite goes, it carries Infinity. That is why the finite is considered to be great. Otherwise, the finite is unreal because it goes through change, death, and decay. Its form and name change. The finite is significant only because it carries Infinity. Nobody wants to keep a body at home that no longer has Infinity within because it will start giving off a foul smell. Nobody says, "He is my father," but rather, "It is my father's dead body." Willingly, everybody parts with it because Infinity is no longer present. They put it in a coffin that would suffocate a living person and bury it.

You are a shrine of the Lord of life. You should be fully aware and conscious of the reality that the greatest of all dwells within you. If you are not aware of that, you will remain insecure and full of fears. The more you have fears, the further away from the Lord you are. You should be confident. There was a time when a mother used to teach her child, "You are Atman. You are great. Don't be sad. There is no reason for you to be afraid. You are going to be great in life. You are going to serve the country. You are going to serve the universe. You are a member of His universe. God is always with you. God is witnessing all your actions."

You are a finite vessel that is carrying Infinity within. You are great because there is something called Infinity in you. You are complete in yourself, no matter how much you condemn yourself or what others say about you. You move because Infinity dwells in you. Without that Infinity you are nothing. You carry that Infinity wherever you go. Even when you are in deep sleep that Infinity is with you. When you are fooling yourself, that Infinity is with you. If God is everywhere, then He is also in you. If He is in you, why are you afraid? You simply have to realize it. You are not realizing it because there is something between you and the infinite Reality that is within you. There are many barriers to cross before you reach the fountainhead of life and light within you. You are not prepared to accept that God can live in such a small person who has so many faults and weaknesses. Your mind creates a barrier. Your thinking does not let you go beyond. There is some power that motivates your mind to think. Why are you not aware of that power? Why do you say the light of the sun, moon, and stars is great? Why do you not see the light within yourself? Just say to yourself, *If there is any living shrine of the Lord, it is I. I am greater than the Lord because I own the Lord in my heart and I am moving everywhere. I am great because He is with me.* This will happen if you are constantly aware of the Reality within you. With this feeling you can enjoy. Learn to work with your mind. Once you start working with yourself, who can stop your progress? When you start examining within try to understand your inner life, your fears, your habits, the way you have trained your mind. Working with the mind means working with your samskaras from the unconscious. Learn to be bold and courageous so you can handle all the past impressions that come forward to disturb you. If your samskaras, your past karmas, are forcing you to do something, you cannot escape. By resisting, you only create more conflict for yourself. You simply have to fathom that level of life and you are there.

How can you individually function in the world, be perfect, and yet be free? The symbol of yoga is the lotus flower that grows in the water, but its leaves remain unaffected. If you keep in your mind that you have come for some time and then you have to go, nothing should bother you. Why attach yourself to the things of the world? As long as they are with you, you should use them. When they are not with you, do not feel sorry for yourself. Remember this and you will not be sad. The world never makes anyone sad. You get attached to the things of the world and then you become sad. If you learn the technique of living in the world and yet remaining above, you will not think that you are incomplete or incompetent. You have all the resources within you. By using the means in the external world and all the resources and potentials that you have, you can attain that which is called *moksha*, freedom, or Self-realization. Learn to live in the world but do not allow yourself to be of this world. Then you can walk on the earth exactly as Christ and Moses walked.

Yoga teaches the philosophy of integration in life. If you use each finger separately, they have no strength. But if you use them together, they become strong. The pillar of integration in life is vairagya. Whether you believe in God or not, learn this. Vairagya is not escape from the world; it is facing the facts of life. Father and son both know that the day will come when one of them will leave. This is truth! I know the day will come when I will leave and you will leave. One of us will leave forever. Knowing this fact, why do you cry? A great poet said, "Parting is a day of meeting. Parting is a day of festivity. Let us celebrate it." In some cultures no one mourns or cries when someone dies. They beat drums and sing songs when they take them to the burial ground. For them, death is not something ugly. It is a festivity. Nothing lives with you forever. If you remain sad and continue to think of someone after his death, you may create problems for that person and unconsciously attract the unconscious mind of that person. If you love someone, let him be happy wherever he is. You should be joyous toward the departed ones, not sad. One who dies is never sad; one who survives is sad because he is selfish. Do not be afraid of death. Just as you take rest, death also gives you rest. Fear of death is not good. You will be more fearful if you do not practice vairagya.

The soul who is trying to cross the mire of delusion and go to eternity has two wings—abhyasa and vairagya. Yoga is not possible if you have not learned abhyasa and vairagya. Whether you are on the path of action or the path of renunciation, it does not matter. You can gain Self-realization if you understand the purpose of life and if you are constantly aware of the center within. The Self is the center, the fountainhead. Once you know the real Self, the Self of all, then you will attain freedom from petty-mindedness and you will no longer be able to hate anyone. The real Self, which is the Self of all, includes all and excludes none. Deep within you is the source, the fountainhead that is the Self of all. When you make your mind inward and one-pointed, and fathom those boundaries that you have created for yourself, you will find all-encompassing love. That love will emanate through your mind, action, and speech.

DESERVE First and Then Desire

People often come to me for instant knowledge, instant samadhi. They say, "I do not want to do anything. Please, Swamiji, give me *ashir-vada* (blessing)." Let me assure you that samadhi is not something that dawns all of a sudden. There is nothing like instant samadhi or instant enlightenment. Many of you think that a guru comes and blesses you and you are in samadhi. This never happens. Many people would like to be enlightened in a second's time without having to do any preparation. If someone has the power to awaken the dormant power of shakti, the primal force of kundalini, how are you going to handle it if you are not prepared? In the path of sadhana, preparation is very necessary. Preparation does not mean making any physical effort. Preparation means becoming aware of another level of consciousness.

Long ago, when I was twenty-seven years of age, I opposed my master. After working hard I could not attain samadhi. I told him, "Please give me samadhi."

He said, "You are not yet prepared for samadhi. If I pour a jug of water in a small bowl, it is of no use." Then he said, "Okay; bring me a bowl."

I brought a bowl. He said, "Give it to me and close your eyes."

He made a hole in the bowl, gave it to me, and started pouring milk in it. Nothing would stay in the bowl.

I said, "Hey, what are you doing?"

He replied, "I am teaching you, but your head is like this bowl! If you have holes in your head, you cannot retain anything."

You should deserve first and then desire. You want to do what you want to do. You want to think the way you want to think. You want to understand the way you want to understand. You are constantly being tossed by your wants and desires and you are completely under their control. How can you be happy? You are blinded and troubled because of your wants. It is difficult for one to cross the boundary of wants. Human beings cannot understand how not to have desires and yet to live, how not to have desires and yet to believe in God. How can you live in the world without desires? What is the fun in that? Want is different from need, and need is different from necessity. Human needs are very few; human wants are millions. If you go toward human needs, every human being can be comfortable. But if you go on fulfilling human wants, there will be no end. If a human being wants to live with necessities, there will be no problem. Instead, he wants and wants and wants, and forgets both his necessities and needs. Sadness means a want that is unfulfilled. All my wants have been fulfilled and I am not sad. I am not so foolish to have a want that is not fulfilled. In my life I had a couple inside me—one was called *want* and the other was called *desire*. They kept on breeding and I could not stop them. One day I decided, *Why should I have a desire that is creating so many problems for me? I will not want anything that will create problems for me. Why should I? If I want something, I should have it. Why keep that desire within me and become sad?* So I selected a few wants and I had them. After having them I found out that I expected too much from them, and they could not give me anything. Wanting, wanting, wanting is not a happy situation. So I stopped. I am careful about wanting anymore because it is not fulfilling. Sadness no longer comes. No one comes and makes me sad. No one has told me to be sad. Who creates sadness? It comes from a bad philosophy of life—bad living, bad thinking, bad desiring. Why should I become sad? I am here to make others cheerful. If I become sad, nobody will ever make me happy. The voice of silence comes from within, *You are not born to be sad.* And I follow that. You can flow tears, but tears of joy, not tears of sadness. So I am never sad. There is no space for sadness in life if you really remember that the center of love and light is within you. If you calculate your whole life, you will find out that you have very little time. Do you want that time to be stolen by sadness? Why should you do this? There is no place for sadness. You have all the things of the world that you need. You have a good home, a good relationship, children; you have enough to spend; you have prestige. Yet you are not happy. You need to apply all the things that you have for something higher. That something higher is called happiness. Happiness is a state of tranquility in which you do not allow anyone to disturb your mind.

One day my master said to me, "I have not given you one more mantra."

I said, "You have not taught me?"

He said, "No. But I would like to do it now."

I felt sad and I said, "You have been hiding things from me."

He said, "Hey, come on. Wake up! Above all the mantras I have given you, finally I give you one mantra. No matter where you live or wherever you go, in whatever condition you are, even while you are crying in pain and agony, remember my words: Learn to be happy. No one can make you happy. No one has the power to insert happiness. There is no such medicine that can make you happy. You have to learn to make yourself happy. No matter where you go, learn to be happy."

Happiness is a state free from all pain and misery. It is not something that you have to gain. You are working and making efforts

for material goals. Happiness is not like that.
Happiness lies within you. It is not outside
you. The outside world distracts you and
dissipates your energy. The outside world
has never given happiness to anybody. But
it cannot be avoided.

If you prepare yourself to know the higher
knowledge, then you will deserve. To deserve means
to increase your capacity. You want to put the entire
ocean in a bucket. The ocean is there. You can have
it, but you do not have the capacity. When you
deserve, you will have the capacity. The Lord, the
Reality, the Truth, is always within you. You simply
have to become aware. You can make sincere efforts
to work with yourself. Don't be disappointed with
failures. When you start to make sincere efforts and
start to practice, you will find light on the path. The
light itself will guide you. The light of consciousness
is within you. If you ignore that light, the guide outside
you, the external teacher, will be of no use to you. He
will make you a slave. Every individual has certain
notions. He also lives with his notions. He creates a
following and millions of people are swayed and
misguided.

Do you know what a guide means? The word
guru has been vulgarized. Such a pious word is being
misused. I call it guide. Do not depend much on guides.
It is better for you to prepare yourself and remain
awake. The scriptures say to wake up from the deep

sleep of ignorance. Remain fully awake, remain conscious, and go on learning. Never close the door of learning. The day you close the door of learning you become ego, ego, ego. In the Himalayas the teacher examines the student and the student examines the teacher. When my master sent me to various teachers he told me, "The teacher who can sit still for a long time is a good teacher because he has practiced something. Listen to him. If the teacher changes his posture many times in five minutes, do not waste your time there."

There are certain signs and symptoms that have been explained by the great scriptures. The scriptures help the student to know who is a good teacher so he does not waste much time. Otherwise, what are we teachers doing? Suppose you want to go to New York. You come to Swami Rama for directions and Swami Rama says to go this way. You meet a different Rama on the way and he says, "Oh, come on! He does not know anything. Go this way." And the student is very sincere. Then another teacher says, "Both Ramas are fools. Better go this way." By that time the poor fellow has wasted twelve years and he is nowhere. The word *teacher* means "knowledge." The knowledge should be followed, not the individual personality of the teacher. The subject should be given prime importance, not the individual. Teachers have complicated things. Yoga science has suffered because of this. One teacher says, "This is my method." Another teacher says, "This is my method." The poor student is confused. After some time he finds that his mind, his individuality, and his pocket have been robbed.

When you become aware of the light within, and that light reveals the Truth to you, there are no chances of being misguided. Teachers come and go. From your external teacher just pick up that which is useful for you and leave that which is not useful. No doubt you need a teacher, a guide. I will never tell you that you should not seek and you should not learn from other people, or that you should not study books. Teachers only inspire you and make you aware of that Self-existence that you have forgotten. Their role is to make you aware of the Reality. You do not need any new form. Christians should not become Hindu, Hindus should not become Buddhist, and Buddhists should not become anything else. They should remain as they are and not create any serious new problems for themselves. A known devil is better than an unknown devil. Remember this. Try to make your life happy wherever you are. Yoga science tells you to go to the inner levels of your being and be guided by the light that is already within you, that leads you in the darkness. If you understand the light within, when you are introduced to that light, you will not crave for any outer guidance. Learn to make your abode in darkness so that you can see the light, but not the superficial light. Superficial light creates problems for you and does not allow you to see the light within. When you start treading the path you will never find any difficulty, for the light is already within you. The light within you is coming out. When I look at your faces I find that they are different because of the light that has the power of discrimination. That light can correctly judge and understand and know. That light is higher than any other light of the sun, the moon, and the stars. That is why human beings are superior to all these lights that you see outside yourself. In the light of the sun, in the light of the moon, and in the light of the stars there is no discrimination. The light within you has the power of discrimination. You can use that light to see the darkest corners of your inner chamber. For that you do not need outer guidance. The purpose of a guide, guru, or teacher is to introduce you to that light.

There have been certain instances of sudden enlightenment like Saul on his way to Damascus. Do you think that it happened all of a sudden? That's not possible; why don't all bad men become St. Paul today? Deep down in his heart of hearts he must have had some desire for Truth. He must have always thought of transforming his personality. In the divine path, desire is a very strong motivation. When Saul was finally fed up with the life of crimes he was leading, that desire came from within and motivated him. He started treading the path to Damascus with the one-pointed thought of purifying his way of life. He became one-pointed and his mind and all of his energy started flowing to the center of consciousness within, and he was enlightened. If you are aware that in this lifetime you have to transform your personality, and you constantly have that thought, nobody can stop your progress. Desire is not part of will. Desire and will are two different things. If your desire is one-pointed, if all your desires are swallowed by one desire, then desire is helpful for attaining samadhi.

Sometimes spiritual desire can also cause problems. If the flame of the desire to attain is burning within you and you are not acting according to your desire, you will remain restless and you will suffer on account of many diseases. You have the desire to attain but you are not working with yourself. You are ignoring the main task of life. If you have a spiritual desire to attain the highest Reality, and if you do not direct your energies toward that, you will go through a series of depressions. You will condemn yourself and you will think that your life is of no use, that you have wasted so many hours, so many days, so many years, and still you have not attained samadhi. Now nothing is going to happen. Death will come, and then you will be reborn again. Because of that desire for enlightenment you are going through depression.

Start studying the sayings of the sages and the scriptures from those great people who really practiced. They are very helpful. Dumb devotion is not good. Devotion is called *bhakti*. Bhakti is a compound of *prema* and *shraddha*, love and devotion, love and reverence. *Bhava* is controlled emotion. When you know how to work with intellect and emotion both, that is a flight from intellect to intuition. It can be explained by a simile.

Two people were going on the same path. One was blind and the other was lame. The one who was lame could see. He said, "Well, blind man. You are so healthy. Where are you going?"

He said, "I am going this way."

The other one said, "I am also going this way, but I am lame."

After discussing they agreed to tread the path together. The one who was blind asked the lame man to ride on his shoulders. The blind man had strong legs and the lame man had very good eyes, so the path became easy then.

Mind and heart should become one. Heart is the center of emotion; mind is the center of thought. When you combine emotion with intellect then you are working with bhava or devotion. Devotion is a combination of two things. You love your girlfriend but you have no devotion toward her. You love God and you have devotion toward God. There is a vast difference. *Devotion* means "love plus reverence." Bhava is that state where you channel your emotions for the higher purpose of life. If your emotions are directed toward a particular point, you can attain the height of ecstasy. When your whole being spontaneously goes to a state of tranquility through music, through art, through the object of your love, through that something that makes your mind one-pointed, you can experience the height of knowledge. Many great sages of the world have experienced the height of wisdom and knowledge because they attained that ecstasy. Mind does not function there. Mind cannot intervene; mind cannot reason; mind cannot say why has this thing happened like this? Emotion, if properly directed, can also be a source of knowledge.

Illumination is attained by devotion toward God. You are devoted to the things of the world so you are in the world. You have chosen to have a world so you have it. This is all your choice. Devotion is very powerful. When you are devoted to something, you get it. You got the world because you are devoted to the world. Now you can change that. With the help of devotion to God, you can attain illumination. *Illumination* here means "spirituality, enlightenment, Self-realization." God within you is capable of giving you freedom and illumination. Remember that you are not only a body, senses, and mind. God is within you. When you realize this you will be enlightened. When you become aware of Reality you will attain illumination. Spiritual *enlightenment* means "freedom from all miseries — physical, mental and spiritual."

Consciousness does not dawn all of a sudden without sincere efforts. If you are tired of efforts and if you do not know what to do next, then grace dawns. The greatest power in the world is the divine power of grace. This happens when you are prepared, when you have done your duties properly, and you have completed all the preliminaries. Grace comes and fills the gap you find in human life. You will find great joy in that which you attain yourself. That which is given to you all of a sudden will be of no joy to you. Even if you do not have a teacher but you make sincere efforts, the time might come when wisdom dawns, exactly as Saul became Saint Paul on the way to Damascus. It happens by the grace of God. That grace comes when you use all your human efforts. That is called the ascending force. When you are tired and you do not find the way, you say, *Now I cannot do anything. I have used all of my resources – my body, with all my little power; my breath; and my limited mind. Now I have reached a plateau.* There dawns that wisdom that helps you, that leads you to the other shore of life.

Sometimes your samkalpa-shakti, your determination, is tested by nature. My master said, "If you can sit in one posture for four hours and thirty-six minutes, you will be in samadhi."

I could sit for more than five hours, but I did not attain samadhi. I said, "Either I am wrong or my master is wrong."

I asked Nirvanji who was wrong, and he said, "Neither your master nor you. Your method is wrong."

I said, "What is that method?"

He said, "I will tell you."

I did not listen to him. I got disgusted and said, "This old man has destroyed my life."

My friends used to write to me, "Where we are we go to the cinema; we go to see dramas; we go out with our girlfriends. Sometimes we drink and dance and sing. What do you do in the cave? How terrible it is for you to live in the Himalayas in the cave, just reading, writing, and meditating—closing your eyes for nothing and wasting your youth. How wonderful it is to drink, to dance, and to live in the world. Will you please let us know what are your experiences?"

I had nothing to share because I was a student doing experiments. I used to tear a page from my copy and write down, "Thank you very much for your letter. I could not find ink to write to you, so do not feel bad that I am writing with pencil. I am still making experiments. The day I find out something I will write to you. Can you let me know in your letter what happens to you when you drink and go out? How do you feel? Do you get good sleep, or do you feel bad, or what do you feel? What have you attained?" I used to put such questions to them.

One day I became very obstinate and the whole night, instead of meditation, I thought of committing suicide the next day. I said, "Look. If I do not attain samadhi tomorrow morning, I am not going to live." The whole night I brooded on this thought. Next morning I went to my master. When you are disgusted and disappointed because of your own weaknesses you become blind.

I said to him, "I want nothing to do with you. You are not my teacher or guru or anything."

He looked at me and said, "What has happened to you? The whole night you brooded on one idea and that was it. 'I would like to commit suicide.' You have strengthened that idea so much that it has completely controlled your life. You have become blind."

I said, "You must be in samadhi. That does not give me wisdom. You told me that sitting in one posture without movement for four hours and thirty-six minutes would lead me to samadhi. I can do it for five hours, but nothing has happened. You promised me samadhi and now you are escaping."

He said, "What do you want to do?"

I said, "I want samadhi or I just want to kill myself. I want to jump into the Ganges."

He said, "Go ahead!"

That hurt me--my father, my master, telling me to go ahead and jump and kill myself.

I said, "I will."

"Please help yourself."

I tied a rope around a big rock.

He said, "What are you doing?"

I said, "It is none of your business what I am doing. I am tying a rope to a big rock and the other end of the rope will be tied around my waist. When I jump the rock will keep me from floating. That is what I am doing."

"Very good idea, son."

I thought, "This man pretended to love me, but he really does not love me."

You know, sometimes you are so egotistical that you can kill yourself for others to preserve your egotistical feelings. This was my condition.

I said, "Goodbye," and I started tying it.

When he saw that he said, "He really can do this. Stay. Wait there for a second!" When he saw my determination, that I was prepared to even die for samadhi, then he said, "Sit down here."

He just touched me, and for nine hours I did not know what had happened to me. I sat for nine hours without knowing where I was. When I came out I was in great delight. That tap reminds me to go to that state again, and it is not difficult. What did he do? At that time my mind was one-pointed. He twisted that one-pointed desire. I did not wish to have anything of the world. I wanted only one thing — samadhi. I have one thing today because of that touch. I can sit for nine hours without any problem, without dis-ease, in great comfort, in great joy. That is what I got.

There is something called *shakti-pata* that a teacher gives. It is not the mass hypnosis that people use for a gimmick. A guru can give shakti-pata to his prepared disciples. The ascending force comes when they have prepared themselves, utilizing all human potentials. Finally he touches them. What is his touch? The descending force or grace. It is possible, but you have to prepare yourself.

The guru is he who has dispelled the darkness from his mind and heart. Guru knows about the mysteries of life here and hereafter, and what world means. Guru knows the difference between the little *I* and the real *I*, the nonself and the true Self, the mere self and the real Self. Such a teacher has the power to lead those students who are prepared, who have the desire, and whose lamp is ready. He has simply to light the lamp with the touch. That touch is important. Such people are rare who can do it.

Where is there place for grace when there is a law of equality? When you have done your efforts with mind, action, and speech, even then you may not be successful. Then you cry like Kanva, a great rishi of the Vedas. He is called Kanva because he used to cry bitterly, "I have made all efforts and I have not attained anything, my Lord." Suddenly the field of mind expanded and he went beyond the unconscious to the domain of peace and happiness within.

Most of you believe in God according to your convenience. When you want something and that something is not being attained or achieved by any other way, you call, "Oh, God. Help me!" Once you receive help, you forget God again. Grace through human effort is called the ascending force. When the ascending force meets the descending force that is called *kripa* — blessings or grace. Grace plays a great part in our lives. Grace is of four types: the grace of God is of course great; the grace of teacher is also important; the grace of the scriptures that you study; and finally, the grace of self. If you do not have grace of self, these other three graces will not work.

My master told me, "I have been repeatedly teaching you, but you do not assimilate it. You have my grace, you have the grace of God, you have the grace of the other swamis, and you have the grace of the scriptures. You lack your own grace."

Any human being who gives all responsibility to the Lord, gives away his own responsibility, and cripples his human potentials. If you don't want to perform your duties and then say, "God will do everything for me," this is not good. You are not utilizing the gifts given to you by Providence. When you do not use human effort yet you believe in God, God says, "No. Human effort is a gift given by Me. Use it." When a human being does not use the gifts given by God he is depriving himself. If He has given you eyes but you close your eyes and start walking, God says, "No. This is not right. Pay full attention when you walk. Do not blindfold yourself and stumble and get hurt."

Human potentials are immense. When you discover them you will find that you have tremendous power. The more you explore, the more you will be amazed and the more you will come to know that you are not as small as you have been thinking you are. You always leave your progress in the hands of the Lord and you think you do not have to make human efforts. Your enlightenment is not in the hands of the Lord; it is in your hands. How far can human effort lead you and help you? You can become a perfect human being. A perfect human being is one who has attained the state of samadhi, the highest level of consciousness. Consciousness is that loving light that flows spontaneously on various grades and levels and enables you to know and see and understand things in the external world. Consciousness is the finest expression and manifestation of the Absolute Reality that you have within you. People think there are states of enlightenment or consciousness as there are states of mind. There are not. Consciousness is singular. There cannot be various states of consciousness, but there are various levels. When mind starts traveling on various levels, then mind knows that consciousness at one level is dim, and then it becomes clearer. Finally it is going toward perfection. Now it is perfect. These are the levels. You should not say that consciousness is a state of mind. Mind is a different thing from consciousness. Consciousness is *chetana*. Mind is a traveler who wants to travel to the highest level of consciousness. When you purify the mind and make the mind one-pointed, then mind can attain that level of consciousness. Some of the books describe that it flows both ways—downward toward darkness, upward toward light. If you can allow your mind to travel upward, then you will know the highest level of consciousness.

Once the River has Met THE OCEAN, There is No Way of Going Back

When you attain a state of samadhi, what will happen to you? The day that you attain a state of samadhi, not only will you stop identifying yourself with the objects of the world, but you will be established in your essential nature. You will become a yogi. Your mind, actions, and speech will be guided by pure consciousness and you will no longer commit mistakes. You will not hurt, harm, or injure anyone in any way. You will become more creative, dynamic, and selfless, and you will understand the meaning of life. Once you have attained the highest state of tranquility you will not be affected within by worldly turmoil and worldly situations. Many of you wonder if you are in samadhi, can you still lead a married life? Definitely. Will you still be fit for the world? All the great rishis and seers, except for a fortunate few, were married. They lived a long life and they were great teachers in the world. It is not easy to remain a bachelor. Those who are wedded to their philosophy can lead a married life and yet can attain samadhi. I have five teachers and they were all householders.

I was sent to study and to practice yoga from a *grihastha* (householder), not from a swami. From a swami you can learn the Vedas and wisdom but you cannot learn yoga unless he has learned from a right source. It was near Ghazipur, the place I visit whenever I find time. From Banaras you go toward Ballia and there is a place called Tiwadipur. That is my real temple in India. When I am in the mountains I go to the monastery; in the plains I go to that place.

This great man was a householder who had three sons and two daughters. He had met a guru who had taught him Patanjali's yoga system and he used to meditate. His name was Anandapandeji. I stayed with him and learned from him. He had a little cottage on the banks of the Ganges. In India there are often floods in the Ganges and when a flood comes it is devastating. We have different seasons — summer, winter, and rainy season. Rainy season means it rains all the time in torrents. After the rains had started in rainy season he said, "Look, son. Now I will be absolutely devoting my time for samadhi." He was sixty-six years of age. "You can go and come back after some time. Lock this door and leave me alone. I don't need food, water, or anything."

He had that wisdom that we call *jada* samadhi — when you have very little to do with your body and you really remain above, yet in the world. What happened? Next day, by chance, a flood came and swept away that small thatched cottage. That flood lasted for seven days and I was very worried. I searched for him and found him after five days, thirty-six miles away from that place, seated under a tree. Half of him was buried in the mud. The currents of water had pushed him onto the bank, and he was seated in the same position under a tree. He was still in samadhi.

I took him like that, put him again in a small cottage far away in the village, and after three months he opened his eyes.

He had five children. It is not necessary for you to become a priest or a swami, or to leave and renounce the world, ignoring your duties. You have to regulate your life, perform your duties properly, understand your energy levels, understand how much to speak and why you are speaking, and how much work you can do. Are you overdoing or are you becoming lazy and inert? Are you becoming irresponsible? If you understand something about the external world, you will get enough time and you can devote that time to know the higher knowledge and attain samadhi.

There is a samadhi that is called negative samadhi. When you are in deep agony, that deep agony can lead you to a state like samadhi. But that is not samadhi. When you worry too much and go into a deep coma-like state that cannot be called samadhi. Many people are in a coma, but they are not in samadhi.

Sometimes you might think that you are in samadhi when you are not aware of your body or individuality. Are you in samadhi? You are not. If you have received a hunch by chance, are you in samadhi? You are not. If you are clairvoyant, even then you are not in samadhi because you are not in touch with the Reality. In samadhi you are one with the Reality.

Once I went to Ceylon for three months and when I came back to Rishikesh where I had my present ashram I found a great swami there. Many new shops and stalls had been put up and everybody was selling malas and this and that. I said. "What has happened in my absence? From where has this swami come?"

They said, "He is a great sage."

I looked at him and said, "Who is this sage?"

I knew many great yogis. I recognized him. He was my *dhobi* (washerman)! He had only one donkey and nothing else. He had lost that donkey and in his grief he had become completely unconscious. People thought he was in samadhi. Those who wanted to exploit him became his disciples and started worshipping him and taking money from others. He stayed in that state for seven days. The moment he woke up, people thought some wisdom would come out of his mouth. Do you know what he said? "Where is my donkey?"

Samadhi is often compared with sleep and is considered to be very near to sleep. If you really want to understand something about samadhi, you should first understand something about sleep. There is a very fine demarcation between sleep and samadhi. During sleep you are very close to Reality, yet you are not aware of Reality. A great sage and a person who is in deep sleep are both there with Reality. The sage is aware of Reality, but the person who is sleeping is not aware. If you can retain consciousness while you are sleeping, that is samadhi.

From a practical viewpoint, Patanjali accepts sleep as a modification of mind, though in reality it is a state of mind. Mind goes through three states — waking, dreaming, and sleeping. When you are fast asleep you are not conscious of your body or of those persons with whom you are attached, or of your wealth. While you are sleeping you are not at all attached to anything. Are you then in samadhi? You are not. In deep sleep you are not aware of the Truth, though you are very near. In samadhi you are constantly aware of the Truth. In samadhi you are fully awake. Samadhi is perfect rest or sleepless sleep. You are fully awake, yet you have the power to go to the deeper state where you can obtain rest exactly as you obtain during sleep. You remain fully conscious and fully aware. Mind has to be trained to go to the fourth state, turiya, or sleepless sleep, a state beyond the sleeping state. Yoga-nidra is not turiya. It is a little bit below turiya, between sleep and turiya. The state of samadhi is much higher than sleep. In samadhi you experience the deepest level of consciousness. You are not under the influence of the inertia of sleep.

Sleep does not transform anyone's personality. You sleep every day and nothing happens to you. It does not solve your problems nor does it change your attitude. Samadhi transforms your personality. A fool goes to sleep and comes out as a fool in the morning. If a fool goes to samadhi, he will come out as a sage. This is the difference between samadhi and sleep. Samadhi transforms the personality, while sleep does not change anything.

There are varieties of samadhi explained by Patanjali: *samprajnata samadhi* (samadhi with content), *asamprajnata samadhi* (samadhi without content), *savitarka samadhi, avitarka samadhi, savikalpa samadhi, nirvikalpa samadhi, sabija samadhi* (samadhi with seed), *nirbija samadhi* (samadhi without seed), and finally, *kaivalyam*, the Absolute One, when you are free. Purusha finds himself completely free from the clutches of prakriti. You can do that. You can practice and do that.

The first step of samadhi is called samprajnata samadhi. In the first state of samadhi still there is content. You maintain awareness of "I" within, of your individual existence. You are aware of the ocean, that you are a wave in the ocean, yet you are separate from the ocean. You become aware that you are a part of the whole, yet you are different from the whole. You exist with your "I."

In asamprajnata samadhi the difference is this: in the first step of samadhi you realize the bliss, yet you still remain aware of your individuality and your mind still functions on reasoning. In the highest state of samadhi you expand your consciousness and you become universal. You become one with the Absolute.

Sabija means "samadhi with seed." You are very close to Reality but yet you haven't attained that. Mind still stands as a wall between you and Reality. In sabija samadhi, after you have gone beyond many states of mind, you come to the final part of the mind where impressions remain. You are receiving images through your sensations all the time and those sensations are being recorded in your unconscious in the bed of memory, the reservoir of all the merits and demerits of your life. Those impressions are in two states — dormant and active. In sabija samadhi, when you have achieved concentration, when you have attained meditation and gone beyond meditation, those latent impressions come forward and create obstacles for you. Though you are very close you have not yet attained that which is your highest goal. Sabija samadhi is not the final stage of samadhi, which is called nirbija samadhi.

Nirbija means "without seed." *Sabija* means "with seed." In sabija samadhi there are still impressions in your mind. You presume that you have perfectly controlled and purified your mind and that your mind is no longer a source of obstacles for you. You are not aware of those latent impressions until suddenly they come forward from the bed of memory and disturb you. When you start to attain perfection, the latent impressions come forward. Even if you have control over the lower mind and you attain the lower stages of samadhi, there are still conflicts that persist in latent form. You have yet to attain another step called nirbija samadhi, samadhi without seed.

In the first chapter Patanjali explains the whole science for the first class students, those students who have known life within and without, those who have understood life very well and are fully prepared. The key point for first class students is to understand and to control mind and its modifications. Without controlling mind and its modifications you will be identifying yourself with the objects of the world. If you have known the modifications of your mind and have control over them, then you will know your true nature. By having control you will not create obstacles for yourselves, you will be free from all pains and miseries, and you will attain a state of perfect equilibrium and tranquility. Patanjali's system explains the various ways and methods to accomplish this.

Patanjali says if you tread this path systematically, you can attain the highest state of wisdom called samadhi. Such a person is very useful for society. Such a person can guide society and is a blessing to society. Blessed are those who want to attain samadhi, those who are trying to attain samadhi, and those who have attained samadhi. Such persons live like kings of the world. They do not remain in the world of illusion. They are free from problems, attachments, and boundaries. All others live like fools.

When you understand the modifications of mind and try to train all the modifications of mind, and understand how they are related and how to coordinate them, then attaining samadhi becomes very easy. All the decisions that you make will be accurate. Anything you do will be fruitful and you will be free from all pains and miseries. You will be free from the darkness that is called ignorance. Lack of knowledge is ignorance. Lack of light is darkness. Darkness has no existence of its own; ignorance has no existence of its own.

You talk a great deal about free will. You want to know how much free will can be used. You can develop your free will to any extent, according to the laws of karma. There is nothing like free will if you know how to do your karmas. By doing your karmas selflessly you can get freedom from the bonds of karma. Karmas do not bind, but the fruits of your actions give you bondage. When you start doing karma for the sake of others, and you surrender the fruits of the karmas, you will be free from the bondage of the karmas. Such great people do karma according to their free will.

Once I asked my master, "What is free will?"

He said, "I will tell you. Go and stand there. Lift one leg." So I lifted it.

He said, "Now will you please lift both legs?"

And I could not. He said, "First learn to stand on one leg. Then later on you will find the human potential."

I can stand on one leg. That is free will. I cannot stand if I lift both legs. You have free will and you do not have free will. Fifty percent of your destiny is in your hands, and fifty percent is with Providence. As a human being you have fifty percent power, not one hundred percent. The other fifty percent you will have to acquire and accept. If you want to improve, fifty percent is in your hands. The other fifty percent will descend, and that is grace.

Once you have control you will know your essential nature and you can have complete free will. You can float if you want. A drop of water has all the qualities of the ocean. It needs union. You are like a drop of water, and the ultimate Truth, or God, is like the ocean. You simply have to learn how to unite the drop of water with the ocean. You need to meet to become one. Many of you are afraid of losing your individuality when you meet the ocean. No. You do not lose anything. Your individuality is expanded; you become the ocean. Once the river has met the ocean, there is no way of going back. You cross the boundaries of individuality and attain cosmic consciousness in which you become one with Reality.

Expansion is life. Expansion of consciousness comes by being constantly aware of the Truth. *Reality is in me. Reality is in me. Reality is in me.* Finally you will find that Reality alone exists. Then you will see Reality everywhere.

You always want to know how long it will take to attain samadhi. A room that has been dark for many years can be lit up in a second's time; it depends on how intense your desire is. If you are ready and you have a burning desire within, you can enlighten yourself in a second's time. If you have a sincere desire, you can do it. If you are not ready, it will take some time to gather together the wick, the oil, and the lamp. But once you have prepared yourself, you can achieve this ultimate goal.

Appendix A

Sleep

In 1970 researchers at the Menninger Foundation in Topeka, Kansas, spent several weeks examining an Indian yogi, Swami Rama of Rishikesh and the Himalayas. The swami could voluntarily maintain his production of theta and delta brain waves. Theta waves (four to seven cycles per second) often appear when a person becomes drowsy and eases toward sleep; delta waves (about one per second, with very large amplitude) are usually associated only with deep sleep. During one five-minute test, Swami Rama demonstrated theta waves 75% of the time. The next day he deliberately produced delta waves for 25 minutes; he appeared asleep and even snored gently, but afterward he could repeat almost perfectly things said in the room at that time.

(From *1973 Britannica Yearbook of Science and the Future*. Excerpted from: "The Psychic Boom" by Samuel Moffat. Encyclopedia Britannica, Inc. William Benton, Publisher. Chicago, Toronto, London, Geneva, Sydney, Tokyo, Manila, Johannesburg. p. 111).

Tumors

One day Swami and I began discussing tumors. I explained our research with blood flow control and mentioned my idea that, because the vascular "tree" in tumors includes smooth muscles in blood vessel walls — which are presumably controlled from a hypothalamic center — it seemed reasonable to hypothesize that tumors could be volitionally starved through blood flow control and reabsorbed by the body.

"Oh yes," Swami Rama said, "all of the soft tissues of the body are easy to manipulate."

I asked what he meant. He jumped up and said, "Press on this muscle with your thumb." It was a large volume of muscle in the right buttock, the gluteus maximus, just behind the hip bone. He said, "Do you feel any lumps in there?" I said, "No." Then he said, "Wait just a second," and he turned his face to the left, away from me, for three or four seconds. Then he said, "Feel it again."

I pressed the muscle again and discovered a lump about the size of a bird's egg in the muscle. I said, "What is that, a tense muscle, a charley horse?"

The Swami said, "No, it's a cyst." I asked, "What's in it?" He said, "I don't know." "Would you be willing to have it X-rayed?" After a pause, he said, "I don't know. My teacher said that it was possible for X-rays to make changes in cells that I might not be able to control." I said, "How about a biopsy?" He replied, "Maybe."

Then he said, "Feel it again." I pressed the muscle again and the lump was gone. I said, "It's gone." He replied, "Just a second. I will make another one." He looked to the left side again for three or four seconds, then said, "There's another one." I pressed again with my thumb and found another lump, but in a different place — up against the hipbone. It was vertically longer and also narrower, and as I pressed it against the bone it slipped this way and that, as might be expected of a cyst.

It was unfortunate that this demonstration was not done in the laboratory, where medical doctors would have been available to give their opinions. To me, it seemed to be a striking example of mind body coordination.

I asked the swami if he could produce such a cyst in an area that would be easier to observe. Yes, he said, when he was in Germany he had produced a cyst several times on his wrist for physicians. He showed me a small scar. He had given permission for them to excise one of the cysts, which they still had in Germany in a bottle. I asked what the doctors said to him when he manufactured cysts suddenly like that. "They said, 'Swami, you are a very unusual man!' The Swami continued with a disgusted expression, "I was trying to tell them something and all they said was, 'Swami, you are a very unusual man.' They did not think about what it meant."

(Excerpted from: Green, Elmer and Allyce, *Beyond Biofeedback.* Knoll Publishing Company, Inc. 1977. 5th Printing, 1989, pp. 210-11).

Appendix B

Sleep Exercise

Breathe deeply, to your fullest capacity, lying first on the left side, then lying on the right side, and then on your back in shavasana. Use a pillow to keep your head a little higher than the rest of the body, otherwise gastric problems will come and you may think you have a heart problem. Every abdomen by nature creates gases. Particularly those who have a sluggish liver or digestion may have such problems. The pillow should be soft, but the bed should be hard. If you do not use a hard bed, your spine will suffer. First lie down on the left side and close your eyes. The right nostril will open and it will give you extra warmth and energy to digest your meal. Pay attention to the movement of your abdomen. Now exhale and inhale. Do not overdo; it should be natural. Continue to exhale and inhale. Do not retain the breath; there is no retention in this practice. Exhale and inhale ten times. Next, lie on the right side to give rest to the heart, and exhale and inhale ten times. After this, lie on the back in shavasana. Using diaphragmatic breathing, count ten exhalations and ten inhalations. Exhale as though you are exhaling from the head to the toes, without any interruption or jerkiness. If you create jerks, you will disturb your heart. When you are exhaling and inhaling, do not make any noise. The breath should be smooth and silent. If any part of the body is aching, when you are exhaling, mentally go to that part and feel as though you are breathing through it. You will find that your pain is gone. When you are exhaling you are releasing carbon dioxide. You can coordinate the mind with the breath by exhaling all mental tensions with the breath. When you have exhaled, you are empty, and after you empty something, you fill it. Here and everywhere there is energy. You are inhaling gradually from the toes to the head. Do this ten times. By that time, you will be totally relaxed and you will sleep. Consciously do this breathing exercise. First on the left side, then the right side, and finally on the back in shavasana.

Counting Exercise for Improving Memory

Lie down in shavasana, the corpse posture. Make sure that you are comfortable. Withdraw your awareness from the external world. Relax from head to toe and from toe to head with the help of deep breathing. Then count from one to one thousand, and then from one thousand back to one. The day you can go up to one thousand and come back from one thousand to one without being influenced by sleep, you will have attained something. This is a tested exercise. If you do not have enough time, you can lie down and do it up to a hundred.

Visualization Exercise for Improving Memory

Part I

This exercise involves visualizing the letters from A to Z. It is important to use the conscious mind with the movement of the eyes while drawing the letters from A to Z. It has been proven that this process of visualization and exercise is very helpful for improving memory, for bringing home the dissipated, distracted mind. Also, those who want to improve their eyesight can do so with this exercise. The mind and the eyes participate in this exercise. This is not a gaze. Initially, this visualization is done with open eyes. With one arm raised and outstretched, begin to draw the letters of the alphabet in one continuous train. The movement of the arm and hand is closely followed with the eyes and the mind. When you are doing this practice for improvement of the eyesight, you should draw and visualize the letters very large so your eyes are moving a good deal. If you regularly practice this exercise, you will have very good eyesight and at the same time it will be helpful for the mind. If you can draw all the letters properly without any break, then you have done concentration. Many times you will find that your mind slips away. For example, it forgets to draw K and goes to L straight away. Then you should come back. This means you have not organized yourself.

If you train a child to do this, you will find that the child will become immensely powerful. This is only one exercise of many. This exercise can be learned in seven days. It only requires some practice. You will even have control over the movement of your eyes. This has proven to be very good for absentminded persons and for those who have loss of memory.

Just watch how many times your mind slips from the train of drawing A to Z. You can do it in Urdu or Hindi also. I remembered all the alphabets very easily by doing this exercise. Eventually, you will be able to do this exercise with your eyes closed and keeping your eyes still.

Part II

Quietly sit down with your head, neck, and trunk straight, and your eyes closed. Try to locate any muscle tension from the forehead to the toes. Slowly move from the forehead, locating any muscle tension, going down to your toes and coming back. Go down again and locate any muscle tension and come back again. One foot in front of you mentally visualize a candle with a white base and a blue light burning. Now, exhale from the crown of the head exactly to the candlelight, and inhale from the candlelight to the crown of your head. If you cannot imagine a blue light, do not worry. Don't make any effort. Very subtle sound vibrations are coming from within. Just listen to them. Exhale and inhale again. Go to the candlelight mentally while exhaling, and come back again to the crown of your head by inhaling, without any retention. When you have completely inhaled, start visualizing A to Z on the space between the two eyebrows as you are exhaling. Again inhale and exhale smoothly. Now visualize A to Z only. Again pay your attention towards your breath. Inhale, exhale and inhale. Ask your mind to listen to the sound vibrations coming from your pineal gland center. Exhale deeply and inhale again. Gently open your eyes. When you can visualize the letters of the alphabet mentally, when you can draw them mentally, that is called visualization. It is very difficult to visualize something, but once you understand the process, it becomes easy.

Index

About the Author

Swami Rama was born in the Himalayas and was initiated by his master into many yogic practices. His master also sent him to other yogis and adepts of the Himalayas to gain new perspectives and insights into the ancient teachings. At the young age of twenty-four he was installed as Shankaracharya of Karvirpitham in South India. Swamiji relinquished this position to pursue intense sadhana in the caves of the Himalayas. Having successfully completed this sadhana, he was directed by his master to go to Japan and to the West in order to illustrate the scientific basis of the ancient yogic practices. At the Menninger Foundation in Topeka, Kansas, Swamiji convincingly demonstrated the capacity of the mind to control so-called involuntary physiological processes such as the heart rate, temperature, and brain waves. Swamiji's work in the United States continued for twenty-three years, and in this period he established the Himalayan International Institute.

Swamiji became well known in the United States as a yogi, teacher, philosopher, poet, humanist, and philanthropist. His models of preventive medicine, holistic health, and stress management have permeated the mainstream of western medicine. In 1993 Swamiji returned to India where he established the Himalayan Institute Hospital Trust in the foothills of the Garhwal Himalayas. Swamiji left this physical plane in November, 1996, but the seeds he has sown continue to sprout, bloom, and bear fruit. His teachings, embodied in the words, "Love, Serve, Remember," continue to inspire the many students whose good fortune it was to come in contact with such an accomplished, selfless, and loving master.

Himalayan Institute Hospital Trust

Perhaps the most visible form of Swami Rama's service to humanity is the Himalayan Institute Hospital Trust (HIHT). HIHT is a nonprofit organization committed to the premise that all human beings have the right to health, education, and economic self-sufficiency. The comprehensive health care and social development programs of HIHT incorporate medical care, education, and research. The philosophy of HIHT is: love, serve, and remember.

The mission of the Trust is to develop integrated and cost-effective approaches to health care and development that address the local population, and which can serve as a model for the country as a whole, and for the underserved population worldwide. A combined approach in which traditional systems of health care complement modern medicine and advanced technology is the prime focus of clinical care, medical education, and research at HIHT.

HIHT is located in the newly formed state of Uttaranchal, one of the underdeveloped states of India. A bold vision to bring medical services to the millions of people in northern India, many of whom are underprivileged and have little or no health care, began modestly in 1989 with a small outpatient department. Today it is the site of a world class medical city and educational campus that includes: a large state-of-the-art hospital offering a full range of medical specialities and services, a holistic health program, a medical college, a school of nursing, a rural development institute, and accommodations for staff, students, and patients' families. This transformation is the result of the vision of Sri Swami Rama.

For information contact:

Himalayan Institute Hospital Trust,
Swami Rama Nagar, P.O. Doiwala
Distt. Dehradun 248140, Uttaranachal, India
Tel: 91-135-412068, Fax: 91-135-412008,
hihtsrc@sancharnet.in; www.hihtindia.org